Professiona**s and**
Techniques **Series**

Touch-Up & Dent Repair

A mini-course for the do-it-yourselfer
who wants to learn how to do it right.

Do-It-Right Publishing, Inc.
Van Nuys, California

Published and distributed by

Do-It-Right Publishing, Inc.
Post Office Box 839
Newhall, CA 91322-0839

Written by: Michael Bishop
                     Dennis Holmes
                     Brad Zimmerman

Series Concept
& Design by: Dennis Holmes

Production by: Steve Janowski

Photography by: Michael Bishop
                     Patrick Holmes
                     Brad Zimmerman

Illustration by: Steve Amos

FIRST EDITION
First printing, 1991
Second printing, 1992
Third printing, 1993

Library of Congress Card Number: 91-71746

ISBN 1-879110-18-0

Proudly printed in the United States of America.

10 9 8 7 6 5 4

FOREWORD

This book covers some of the most important and money-saving jobs that DIYer's can do: touch-up painting and dent repair. You don't need mechanical skills to do these jobs. And we assume you have no experience in automotive painting or bodywork. But the big asset you do bring is patience, care about the quality of the outcome of the job, and a good dose of your own time!

Using commonly available plastic body filler (widely known under the "Bondo" brand name), a few inexpensive hand tools, and aerosol spray primer and paint, you can easily save several hundred dollars on even one small dent repair!

And the money you earn doesn't stop there. Since the appearance of a vehicle is so important at resale time, your DIY labor is putting money in the bank. You will enjoy the improved appearance of your car or truck while you drive it, and you will get more money for it when the time comes to trade it in. Pretty nice benefits for some careful, enjoyable DIY work!

This book is limited to the easiest and most common DIY body repair and painting projects: touching up paint chips, repairing parking lot rash, and fixing small to medium-sized dents. It does *not* cover the procedures for a full paint job or major collision repair.

A major goal of this book is to teach you the methods and "secrets" of professional bodymen and painters. Their goals are the same as yours: top quality results in the shortest possible time. Our method of teaching is simple: using hundreds of photos, we show you a number of actual repair and painting projects that are typical of those you will encounter.

The detailed level of step-by-step explanation is not common in this type of book. But we think you will find it a pleasant way for learning the techniques, tips, and shortcuts used by professionals—it's like looking over their shoulder as they explain what they're doing.

Be sure to read the *Pro Tips,* which are scattered through the book. These are tidy treatments of important subjects that relate to quality bodywork and painting. The tips are aimed at giving you a quick dose of the kind of smarts that pros build up through years of experience.

As with other books in the Do-It-Right *Professional Tips and Techniques Series,* this book gives you a mini-course in an important area of automotive DIY work. It's goal is to build life-long skills that will enable you to produce top-quality results. And while the book is designed so that each section stands alone, we encourage you to read it cover-to-cover for a rich understanding of the subject. We want you to know not only *what* the professionals do, but *why.*

THANKS

Thanks to our partners—Steve McKee, Lonetta Holmes, and John Dawson. They gave us the enthusiastic encouragement we needed to launch this new series of books.

Thanks to Joe Salazar—a show-winning craftsman—for helping us translate his professional perfection to DIY reality. Thanks to Rex Rutherford for his technical review, bringing his 30 years of teaching and body shop experience to the project.

Thanks to Bert Poncher for freely sharing his 25 years of experience in the automotive aftermarket and helping shape the direction of this Professional Tips and Techniques series.

Thanks to Jana Brett for her assistance in cover design. Thanks to Dan Hackett and Karl Anthony for their technical assistance with Ventura Publisher.

Thanks to Nissan Motor Corporation in U.S.A. and Hyundai Motor America for their support and endorsement of our model-specific series of manuals. They have helped validate our highly visual approach to this type of book, and they have made a lot of their customers quite happy in the process.

And thanks to the 35,000+ professional technicians in Toyota, Nissan, Honda, and Hyundai dealerships for whom we have developed factory training programs and manuals over the past 18 years. It was *you* who taught, and we who learned.

IMPORTANT SAFETY NOTICE

Pay special heed to the *warnings* in this book. They are intended to help protect you and your vehicle. When lifting your vehicle, make sure it is securely supported on jackstands before performing any work underneath it. Do *not* rely on the jack that came with your car or truck for safe support.

You should use standard and accepted safety precautions and equipment when handling toxic or flammable fluids. You should wear safety goggles or other protection during cutting, grinding, chiseling, prying, or any other similar process that can cause material removal or projectiles.

Following proper service procedures is essential for your safety and the correct functioning of your vehicle. We believe that the general service procedures in this book are described in such a manner that they may be performed safely and properly on a wide variety of vehicles. However, it is your responsibility to determine the precise applicability of these procedures to your specific vehicle or engine.

Please note that the condition of your vehicle, or the level of your mechanical skill, or your level of reading comprehension may result in or contribute in some way to an occurrence which causes injury to yourself or damage to your vehicle. It is not possible to anticipate all of the conceivable ways or conditions under which cars and trucks may be serviced, or to provide warnings as to all of the possible hazards that may result. Accordingly, because of these conditions which are unknown to us and are beyond our control, our liability must be and is limited to the cost of this book.

If you use service procedures, tools, or parts which are not specifically recommended in this book you must first completely satisfy yourself that neither your safety nor the safety of your vehicle will be jeopardized. All liability is expressly disclaimed for any injury or damage if you fail in any respect to follow all of the instructions and warnings given in any procedure in this book.

Although the information in this book is based on industry sources and experts, it is possible that changes in designs may be made which could not be included here. While striving for precise accuracy, Do-It-Right Publishing, Inc. cannot assume responsibility for any errors, changes, or omissions that may occur in the information presented here.

Contents at-a-Glance

Detailed Contents

Section 1:
Introduction

WHAT THIS BOOK CAN HELP YOU DO

There are two kinds of vehicles on American roads: those that have chips, dents, dings, and scratches—and those that will get them! It's just a matter of time.

Let's face it, no matter how careful you are, it's almost impossible to avoid minor paint and metal damage. But with a little help from this book, you can keep your car or truck looking great in spite of the rigors of the road and the parking lot.

You don't need experience or exotic tools to get really excellent results. All you need is a place to work, some commonly available paint and supplies, and a few tools from your local auto parts store.

This book will teach you professional tips and techniques for touching up minor chips and scratches. You'll learn how to fix dings and dents—even the big ones. And you'll learn how to sand, primer, and repaint those repairs without investing in a spray gun or compressor.

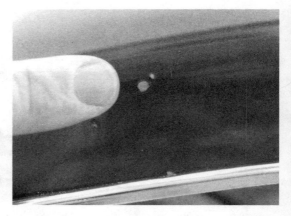

Stone chips and parking lot rash are a good place for you to begin your body work. *Section 3 shows you the techniques for nearly invisible repair.*

A huge selection of automotive spray paint and touch-up paint is available. *You can do much better than just "looking at the color on the cap" to get a precise match. This section shows you how.*

By following the professional tips and techniques in this book, your vehicle can once again have a flawless finish. All it takes is time, a few tools, and the *patience* to do it right!

WHERE AND WHEN TO WORK

Planning the right time and place to work is a big factor in how nicely the job turns out.

First, you need lots of *space*—at least 4 feet all around the area you'll be working on to move comfortably, sand, spray, and paint.

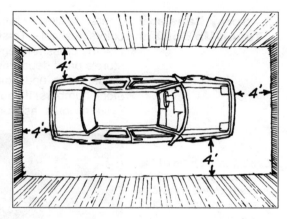

Having enough room to work is essential for good results. Envision the vehicle as a pool table, and then allow enough room to comfortably handle a cue and make your shots.

Second, consider *neighborhood activity.* There's nothing worse than spraying on your final coat of paint, only to have the fellow next door fire up his lawnmower and blow grass clippings into the air.

Third, get an *early start* to avoid afternoon dust and breezes. Usually, the best time for doing a little painting is a weekday morning.

And finally, *weather* is a big factor to consider. The temperature should be between 60°F and 90°F (15°C and 32°C), and the humidity should be below 75 percent. If the forecast includes rain, snow, or extremely low or high temperatures, reschedule your work. You simply won't get quality results on a bad day.

HOW TO MATCH YOUR PAINT COLOR

You will be amazed at the accuracy of modern paint-matching technology. Before you go shopping, *make sure you write down your vehicle's* **color code.** (See the facing page.) This is critical information to ensure a proper paint match.

Spray Cans and Touch-Up Bottles

There are literally hundreds of pre-mixed colors available. To select the correct color, use the cross-reference chart located in the store's paint department. It matches your Model, Year, and Color Number to the paint stock numbers. If you're not sure how the system works, ask for help.

Can't find a bottle of the color you need? No problem. Buy a spray can and shoot a little in a cup. Use this with a brush or toothpick for touching up tiny chips and scratches. We found that a much wider variety of colors are available in spray cans than in touch-up bottles—especially for older vehicles.

Custom-Mixed Paint

If you can't locate the exact color you need, do what the professional painters do: get a can of custom-mix. Automotive paint supply stores are listed in the Yellow Pages. Be sure to take your vehicle color number with you. You can buy as little as one pint of custom-mixed paint, although a quart won't cost much more. Most paint stores use a computer to produce precise results. If you have a custom color, drive the vehicle to the store for a visual match.

PRO TIP: Where to Find Your Vehicle's Color Code

Vehicle manufacturer color codes are shown on the VIN (vehicle identification number) tag. (The VIN is the same long ID number that's on your registration form.) The VIN tag also contains other information such as model, date of manufacture, assembly plant, and interior trim code as well as the color code.

There is no overall standard location for VIN tags. Different manufacturers locate them in different places. The two illustrations below show you where to look, for almost any vehicle. (If you have a Volkswagen, check first under or behind the spare tire.)

Some vehicles have the VIN tag located in the driver area such as the door posts (A), inside door edges (B), glove compartment (C), and left front body pillar (D).

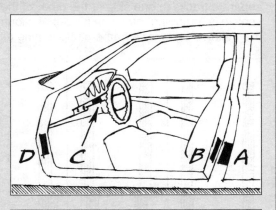

Other manufacturers locate the VIN tag in the engine compartment, on the firewall (E) or (G), under the cowl (F), left-front inner fender (H), left wheel housing (I), or radiator core support (J) or (K).

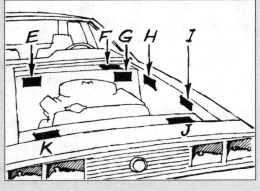

Touch-Up & Dent Repair

PRO TIP: Got a Frame Alignment Problem?

Sometimes a "too-close encounter" causes frame misalignment problems. This is particularly likely if the impact was severe enough to badly damage a bumper or fender. Unibody designs (all front-wheel-drive cars and some rear-wheel-drive compacts) are more susceptible to this type of damage than full-frame vehicles.

The simplest way to check frame alignment is with a little water and a good eye. Wet down about 25 feet of roadway, drive through straight and slow, then examine the tire tracks. The rear tracks should overlay the front tracks evenly. If the rear tires leave separate tracks to one side or the other of the front tracks, your vehicle is "crabbing" because it's out of alignment. It's time to check the Yellow Pages for a frame-straightening expert.

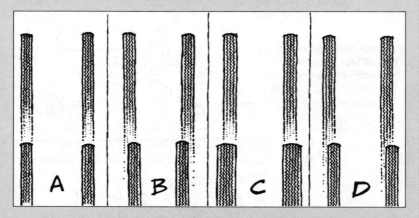

Don't confuse differences in front and rear track widths and tire size with misalignment. *Patterns "A" through "C" are all correct. "A" is made by a car with equal front and rear track widths. "B" is typical of a car with a narrower rear track. "C" is made by wider rear tires. "D" is a car that's badly out of alignment.*

BIG JOBS ARE BETTER LEFT TO THE PROS

Although about 90 percent of touch-up work and dent repair can be performed by the average owner, there are still some jobs that are better left to the pros.

This guide has been written for the owner who wants to learn how to perform *minor* miracles—not someone looking for a career in body work. We assume you don't want to straighten a frame or pull a door pillar back into shape.

You won't find hydraulic straightening jacks, welding equipment, or pneumatic chisels in this manual. Nor will you find air compressors, spray guns, and spray booths. If the damage to your vehicle is so extensive that it requires these professional tools, your best bet is to drive or tow it to an auto body shop and let the pros handle the job.

THE HARDEST THING TO LEARN

Of all the tips, techniques, and secrets you'll learn while repairing dents and painting your vehicle, there's one lesson that bears repeating often:

The most difficult step to learn is... *patience.*

Most of the repairs you'll learn require that you perform a step—then wait. Sometimes it's as simple as waiting 15 minutes for primer to dry. Other times it's as tough as holding your horses for a week while the paint cures before you can use rubbing compound and wax to finish the job. But for professional results, be patient—do it right.

CHEAP PRACTICE FOR BUILDING YOUR SKILLS

If you're a beginner, it pays to do a little practice before taking on the job of sprucing up your pride and joy. You'll find great donor parts at the local salvage yard. For less than $20, you can pick up an orphan fender or door that has a few scratches, dings, and dents in it.

Perfect your techniques and make your mistakes on your adopted part. It lets you practice before diving into your vehicle, and you'll build up some confidence before you tackle the real job.

When you're ready to begin work on your own car or truck, you can always take the practice panel back to the salvage yard. Just don't expect them to pay you for it, even though it looks better!

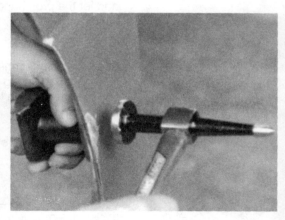

Practice on a slightly battered body panel you get from a salvage yard. It's a great way to practice what you want to do, make mistakes that won't matter, and build confidence before starting on your own vehicle.

Section 2:

Tools and Supplies

The tools, supplies, and paint you'll need to perform minor body and paint repairs are available at local auto parts stores and the automotive departments in major chain stores. Many new-car dealers also carry touch-up paint and supplies.

This section shows you the major items that are needed for a wide variety of jobs. Subsequent sections in this book list the specific items you'll need for a specific job. Since a major goal of do-it-yourselfers is to *save money,* we have selected only inexpensive, readily available tools. Often, you can find these packaged as money-saving kits. Professional results are produced more by the care and patience of your work than by the price of your tools!

SMALL DENT REPAIR TOOLS AND SUPPLIES

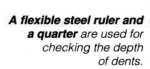

A flexible steel ruler and a quarter are used for checking the depth of dents.

Sandpaper is a big element in body and paint repair. Get a well-rounded selection—a package each of 40, 80, 200, 400, 600, and 1000 grit.

A flexible rubber sanding block is absolutely necessary. We like the ones with sharp spikes or "teeth" that hold the sandpaper firmly in place. (The spikes are under the end flaps.)

A basic body filler "kit" contains filler, hardener, and an applicator. A 1-pint size like this will repair four to six small dents. More complete kits, with sandpaper, primer, spot putty, and a small dent puller are also available. They are best suited for repairing small dings.

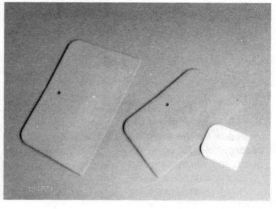

Flexible filler applicators are necessary for applying a smooth thin coat of body filler. Most filler kits have an applicator in the box, and additional applicators are available individually and in sets.

A plastic mixing board is necessary for thoroughly mixing filler and hardener. After mixing, the board holds the filler as you apply it to the repair.

Spot and glazing putty is used on body filler to fill tiny pin holes and imperfections.

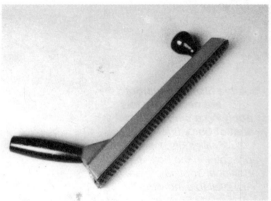

A cheese grater file speeds up the shaping of larger dents. While not absolutely necessary, this tool is a big time-saver on larger jobs.

Terry cloth towels are used for wiping and polishing in many procedures. You'll want to have about a dozen.

FIBERGLASS, ABS, AND RUST REPAIR TOOLS AND SUPPLIES

A standard electric drill motor is used with a sanding disc for rust repair. It's also used to drill holes for a dent puller.

A flexible rubber sanding disc (which is driven by the drill motor) is necessary for sanding off paint and rust.

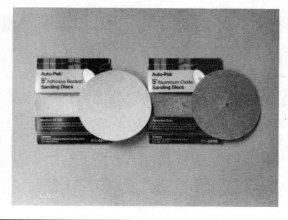

Get a good assortment of circular sanding discs. You'll need 40, 200, and 400 grit. These are used for removing paint and rust—not for final sanding.

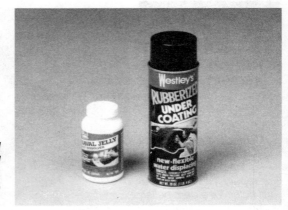

Rust destroyer and converter (or Naval Jelly) dissolves rust. *Undercoating will help keep it away.*

Sheet-metal snips *are necessary for cutting away badly damaged sections of sheet metal.*

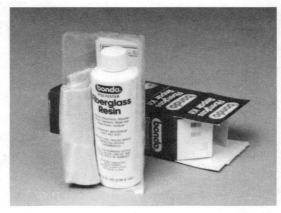

Fiberglass patch kits *come with cloth, resin, and hardener, plus a mixing pan.*

METAL-WORKING TOOLS

There are three basic types of pullers: suction cup pullers, T-handle pullers, and slide-hammer pullers. Each type has its own merits that make it better suited to a particular job. The tools we show you here are the least expensive grade, intended for use by do-it-yourselfers. They are widely available in automotive parts departments and stores.

Suction cup pullers pull on the surface of the dent. *They work best with large, smooth-edge compression dents.*

A small T-handle puller can be used on small dents. *A hole must be drilled in the dent to use this type of puller. We find them much more difficult to control than a slide-hammer puller.*

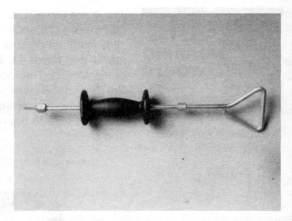

A slide-hammer puller is essential for bigger dents and more complex creased dents. This type of puller screws into holes you drill in the sheet metal. It gives you excellent control. Highly recommended, even for small dents.

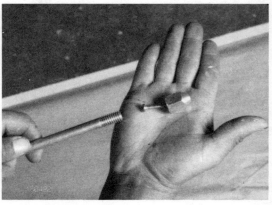

The screw-tip of a slide-hammer puller is just a sheet metal screw. It's easily replaceable. We recommend a smaller diameter screw for most light repairs.

Hammers and dollies are best bought in sets. You get all the types you need for most sheet metal work—all for about $20.

PAINTING EQUIPMENT AND SUPPLIES

Small bottles of automotive paint are used to touch up minor chips and scratches. These bottles include an applicator brush in the cap. Clear coat is available, as well as colors.

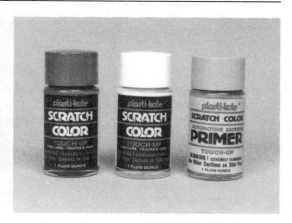

Primer is a must for dent repairs. Two types are available: regular primer and a much thicker "filler" primer. Make sure the type you buy is for automotive use—not household use. If you have a choice of light grey, dark grey, or red oxide, get the color closest to the color of your final paint.

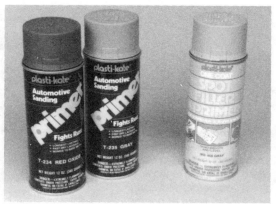

Aerosol cans of automotive paint are required for larger areas. Get the correct color as described on page 4. If you have a clear-coat finish, buy a can of clear-coat for your final layer. You'll also need a can of paint thinner for tool cleanup and removing overspray.

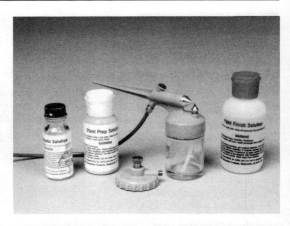

Optional: B&M's air-brush sprayer is powered by the air in your spare tire. This small spray gun can lay down a smooth, clean layer of paint or primer. Inexpensive airbrushes are also available at hobby shops.

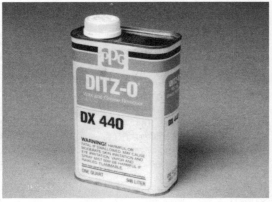

Wax-and-silicone remover (also called wax-and-grease remover) is used to clean the surface you're working on before you apply paint or primer.

This handy tool removes rust from paint-chip craters. If rust isn't removed before touchup paint is applied, rust will soon appear on the surface of the repair.

Masking tape is used to mask trim and other areas during painting. It's also used to hold masking paper in place. Make sure it's "fresh" tape. It should be soft and moist.

Spray painting requires the use of masking paper. Some auto parts stores carry it. If you can't find it there, look in the Yellow Pages for paint suppliers. A regular 1-foot-wide, 50-feet roll is usually less than $10.00. You can also use butcher paper.

A tack cloth is a special dust- and lint-free cloth that is essential for removing dust just before painting. Keep your tack cloth in a sealed plastic bag when not in use to prolong its life.

Rubbing compound or polishing compound is used to bring up the gloss of your final coat of color or clear paint. It can also remove paint overspray that has dried.

Carnauba wax adds the final shine and protects the paint. Use a foam pad applicator to apply it.

100% cotton T-shirt or terry cloth rags are used for rubbing, polishing, and waxing. Don't use a T-shirt that has any writing or graphics on it. Keep your T-shirt rags in large sealed plastic bags to keep them clean when not in use.

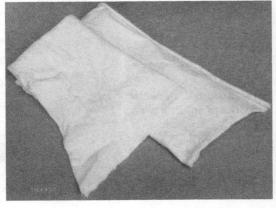

Section 3:

How to Touch Up Chips and Scratches

Minor paint chips and scratches are the easiest type of damage to fix. They're also the easiest to incur. There probably isn't a vehicle on the road with more than 1,000 miles on the odometer that doesn't have at least one paint chip.

The thing that distinguishes a paint chip or scratch from other types of body damage is that there's *no dent in the metal.* The damage is limited to the paint itself.

In this section we show you how to use a toothpick to apply paint to small chips and how to use a small brush on scratches. In Section 10, page 163, we show you a larger, deeper scratch repair project, where sanding and spray painting are required.

Touch-Up & Dent Repair

BEFORE:
Paint chips on the front
are ugly and unavoidable.
Notice how they "draw"
your eye.

AFTER:
Filled and polished. *A*
nearly invisible repair.

Scratches can result from many accidental causes—belt buckles, blue-jean rivets, trees, bushes, and your own door and trunk keys.

Sadly, there is also deliberate scratch damage, called "keying." This form of vandalism gets its name from the act of scratching the paint with a key. It's usually so extensive, even when it's confined to a single panel, that routine touchup techniques do little to hide the scratches. Often, a professional repaint is required. Many auto insurance policies cover "keying" under the

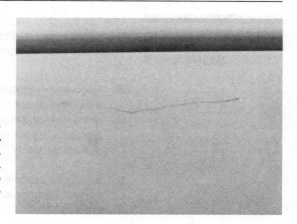

BEFORE:
Door and fender
scratches *are usually caused by carelessly opened car doors and runaway or mispiloted shopping carts.*

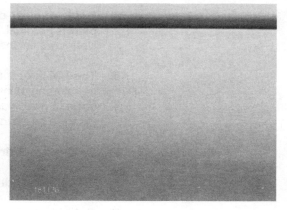

AFTER:
Most scratches are
easily repairable *with correct color matching, a steady hand, careful wet sanding, and patience.*

comprehensive-damage provisions, so check with your insurance carrier if you are faced with repairing this type of damage.

The types of paint chips and scratches we show you how to fix in this section are quick and easy to do—ideal for a beginner. Yet the results are very rewarding. Paint chips attract your eye to them. Making them invisible will really improve the looks of your car or truck.

PRODUCTS AND SUPPLIES

Most of the chip and scratch repair items listed below are available in auto parts stores. Touch-up paint is also available at many auto dealerships.

■ **Wax-and-silicone remover (also called wax-and-grease remover)**—Used to remove wax, silicone coating, and grease, so your touch-up paint will adhere properly.

■ **Bottle of color touchup paint**—See page 4 for how to match your vehicle's color.

■ **Bottle of clear-coat touch-up paint**—For final top coat on repairs to clear-coat finishes.

■ **Toothpick or matchstick**—A "tool" for transferring paint from the bottle to tiny chips. It gives you more precise control than the brush in the cap.

■ **1000-grit wet/dry sandpaper.**

■ **A flexible sanding block.**

■ **Rubbing compound**—A fine abrasive paste to smooth and shine your repair area.

■ **Wax**—Used to seal the repair area and bring it to the same lustre as the surrounding paint.

■ **Two clean 100% cotton T-shirts or terry-cloth towels**—For applying and removing rubbing compound and wax.

SURFACE PREPARATION

The surface in and around a paint chip or scratch must be completely clean and free of any polish or wax so that the touchup paint will stick. A good wax-and-silicone remover will bring you right down to the paint.

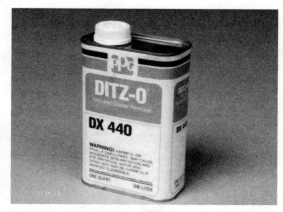

Use wax-and-silicone remover to clean the chip. *This ensures that the new paint will correctly bond to the surface.*

Rub the wax-and-silicone remover around the chip and the area surrounding it. *Wipe the surface with a clean rag, and allow the remover to evaporate.*

HOW TO FILL PAINT CHIPS

Paint chips must be carefully filled with fresh paint, using several thin layers rather than one thick coat. If you have a clear-coat finish, you can make your last layer a clear-coat one, but on repairs this small, it may not be essential. Your goal is to build up the paint inside the crater until it is just level with the surrounding surface.

The easiest way to apply the paint is with the point of a toothpick. It gives you the ability to apply a very small amount of paint to the *inside* of a chip.

Don't brush paint over a chip. *This builds up the area around the chip, along with the chip itself and makes it just as visible as it was before you filled it.*

This is too much paint on the tip of the toothpick. *All that's needed is a very small dab. If you put this much paint in the crater at one time, the paint may soon fall out.*

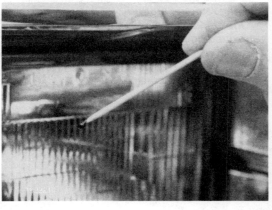

This is the correct amount of paint on the tip of the toothpick. *It will all fit into the crater and not "blob" over onto the surface of the adjacent paint.*

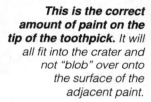

Touch the toothpick to the bottom of the chip crater to transfer the color paint. *Don't spread the paint. Let it gravitate toward the bottom of the crater, then allow it to dry for about 45 minutes.*

Repeat the process one or two more times, until the crater is filled and level with the surrounding surface. *For a clearcoat finish, use color paint for all layers except the final one. If the surface is level, you're done. If you've got too much paint (easy to do), see page 30 for how to wet-sand it.*

HOW TO PAINT A SMALL SCRATCH

Shallow, short scratches (less than an inch long) can be filled using the toothpick technique. Longer scratches are more easily treated with the applicator brush in your bottle of touchup paint or a pin-striping brush. The same rules apply:

1. Apply several thin layers rather than one thick layer.

2. Allow each coat of paint to dry thoroughly.

3. Keep the paint *inside* the scratch—don't let it slop onto the adjacent paint.

Begin by cleaning the area with wax-and-silicone remover followed by a tack cloth. Touchup paint will not adhere permanently to wax.

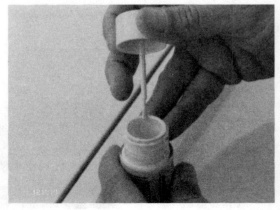

Transfer a small amount of paint to the tip of the applicator brush. The big mistake most amateurs make is using too much paint.

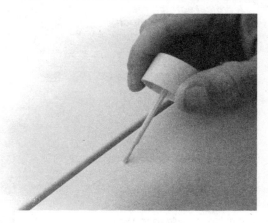

Apply several thin layers of color paint. *Remember, less is always better. Let each coat dry for at least 45 minutes.*

Apply your final coat of color or clear-coat level with the surface. *This is difficult to do perfectly. But at least build a good foundation paint for subsequent wet-sanding.*

Usually, a brushed-on scratch repair will require a bit of wet-sanding to smooth and blend the surface, as shown on the next page.

HOW TO WET-SAND A SMALL PAINT SCRATCH

Let the repaired paint scratch dry for *at least 48 hours* before you do the finishing steps that follow. This curing time allows the paint under the surface to harden and adhere to the primer and surrounding paint.

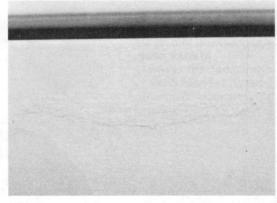

A typical scratch repair with a bit too much paint! To correct it, you'll need to wet-sand the paint down to the same level as the surrounding area.

Use a rubber sanding block and 1000-grit wet/dry sandpaper. Wet the sandpaper with water, and sand the paint very lightly. Use plenty of water! Keep dipping the sanding block in a bucket of water.

Use rubbing compound or polishing compound to smooth and blend the repair. Apply a dime-size dab to a clean cloth, and rub the repair. Rub lightly, and check your progress often. The goal is to blend the repair with the surrounding paint. Before the compound dries, use another clean cloth to remove the film.

Apply carnauba wax and allow it to dry. Buff it out with a soft, clean cloth. The repair should be nearly invisible, with its surface and shine matching the adjacent area.

A more extensive scratch repair and spray-painting job is shown in Section 10, page 163.

Section 4:

How to Fill Small Dings and Dents

INTRODUCTION

Our definition of a "ding" or "dent" is that the body metal has been bent. You can't just paint over these babies, you've got to do some filling, sanding, and aerosol-can painting. Here, you're looking at a few hours of work for some very rewarding results.

The first step in fixing a minor ding or dent is to determine if they really do qualify as "minor." A "minor" dent is shallow enough to be correctly filled without pulling or hammering it out. Deeper dents must be pulled or hammered out before filling. (These techniques are explained in Sections 5, 6, and 7.)

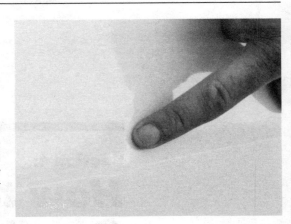

BEFORE:
A good example of a
minor dent. *This little*
door divot can be easily
fixed with filler to bring it
back to the same level as
the surrounding metal.

AFTER:
Filler, primer, and paint
produce almost invisible
results. *This section*
shows you how.

PRO TIP: The 25-Cent Dent Solution

Some dents are too deep (more than 1/4-inch) to be fixed with just filler. If filler is applied too thick over a small area, it can break loose and create cracks around the edges of the repair. It can even completely break loose and fall out of the dent! But it's no trick to quickly assess a dent to see if it can be successfully repaired without pulling or hammering. All you need is a flexible ruler and a quarter.

Set the ruler against the surface, and set the quarter against it, with the word "LIBERTY" centered in the deepest part of the dent. If you can see no more than George's forehead beneath the edge of the ruler, the dent can be fixed with body filler only. This dent does not require pulling.

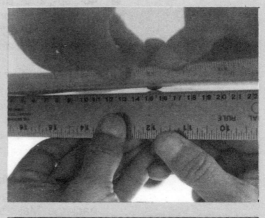

If the dent is so deep that you can see down to the end of George's nose, or farther, use a dent puller to straighten the sheet metal before using filler. Dent pulling instructions are in Sections 5 and 6.

TOOLS AND SUPPLIES

- **Flexible steel ruler and a quarter**—For checking the depth of each dent.

- **Wax-and-silicone remover**—For preparing the surface at several stages of the repair.

- **Several 100% cotton T-shirts or terry cloth rags**—For cleaning and buffing.

- **40-, 80-, 200-, and 400-grit sandpaper**—For removing paint from the dent to prepare the surface, for shaping the body filler, and for finish sanding.

- **Flexible rubber sanding block**—Absolutely essential for a professional, level finish.

- **Mixing board**—For mixing filler and hardener.

- **Plastic body filler with hardener agent**—Sold together in a single package. Make sure your package has hardener.

- **Filler applicator**—For spreading thin coats of filler into dent.

PRO TIP: Understanding Sandpaper Grades

Whether you sand by hand or with an electric drill or sander, the sandpaper grade determines the amount of sanding time. The lower the sandpaper's number, the quicker it works—and the more often you should stop to check your progress.

40- to 80-grit range—With very large and coarse grit, these sandpapers are for removing a large amount of material in a *very* short time. Go slowly and check progress often.

100- to 220-grit range—Still somewhat coarse, they can do lots of damage if used incorrectly. A 100-grit paper removes material quickly and is good for shaping body filler, while a 220-grit is good for scuffing smooth paint to get primer to adhere.

240- to 400-grit range—Used primarily for finishing work, these papers are usually black, can be used wet or dry, and take longer to produce the desired results.

600- to 2000-grit range—Used for extremely fine work, and always used wet. These grits can be used on a painted surface to "color sand" it or remove very small blemishes.

There's a wide range of sandpapers available. Generally, you start with a low number and work your way up.

PRO TIP: Before You Sand, Check Your Available Time

Rock star Neil Young was right when he sang "Rust never sleeps." Before you begin sanding to bare metal, make sure you have enough time to finish the job and cover that bare metal, either with filler or primer. Bare steel, left exposed to air, can develop visible rust in less than 6 hours!

If you're filling one small dent, the procedure will take approximately 2 hours to perform from start to finish. Make sure you don't have to stop at the midpoint and begin again the next day.

Never leave your sheet metal naked. *This job sat overnight, which allowed the rusting process to begin, turning a small project into a large one.*

HOW TO PREPARE THE DENT SURFACE FOR BODY FILLER

One of the keys for fixing a dent is correct surface preparation. You can't just spread body filler over a painted surface. In a few weeks, it will fall out in chunks. And you can't spray primer over existing paint. It won't adhere correctly, and the finish coats of paint won't match the rest of the finish. That's why preparing the surface is so important.

Use a rubber sanding block with 40-grit sandpaper to sand the dent area. The coarse sandpaper will quickly get you down to bare metal.

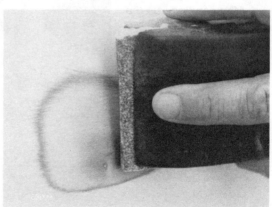

Sand into the center of the dent. You must get down to bare metal for the filler to adhere.

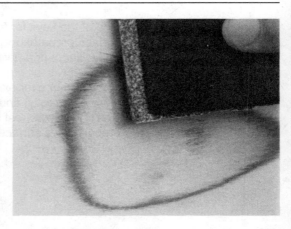

Feather the edges of the repair area with 80-grit sandpaper. *Use lighter pressure to create a smooth transition from the bare metal to the finished paint. Check with your fingers to make sure it is absolutely smooth.*

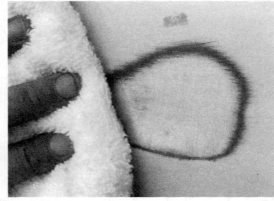

After sanding, rub the surface with a clean rag *to remove all sanding residue and dust. You're ready now to fill the dent.*

HOW TO MIX BODY FILLER

Body filler consists of two elements: filler and hardener. Before being used to fill dents, the two must be thoroughly mixed in correct proportions. Mixing filler correctly is an important secret for getting a smooth finish with minimal spot putty. Incorrectly mixed filler will always produce poor results, with airholes and pits in the surface.

To correctly mix body filler and hardener, you need a mixing board and a mixing tool, like a putty knife, tongue depressor, or ice cream stick.

Stir the filler thoroughly. Before you can apply it, it must be an even color and consistency.

Place a golf-ball-sized glob of filler on your mixing board. This is enough filler for several small dents.

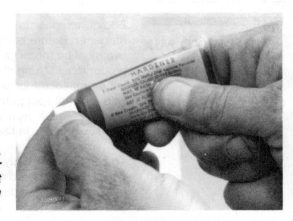

Before adding hardener, squeeze the container repeatedly *for at least 1 minute to loosen and mix it.*

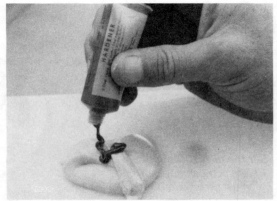

Add a small amount of hardener—about the size of a dime. *The hardener causes a chemical reaction to harden the filler. It's better to start with too little hardener and add more if it's needed. If you use too much hardener, the mixture will set up too quickly, quite possibly before you can apply it to the dent.*

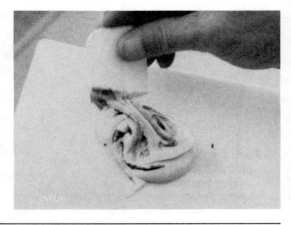

Blend the hardener into the filler. *Use a circular motion to fold the hardener into the filler. You'll see the hardener leave swirl marks when this is done correctly.*

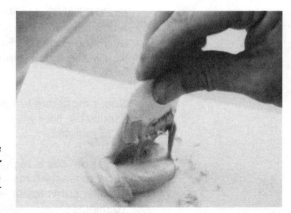

Swirl in both directions to blend the hardener thoroughly into the filler. *Don't lift the applicator as you swirl.*

Push the mixture up into a pile, making small peaks...

...then squash it down, moving it side-to-side. *By going from peaks to pancakes, you'll eliminate air bubbles in the filler. Continue mixing until the filler and hardener are thoroughly mixed and have a single, consistent color. Mixing should take only a minute or two.*

IMPORTANT: *Apply filler to the dent as soon as it's mixed.* In normal temperatures (anything above 68°F), you must apply the filler within 3 or 4 minutes after it's been mixed.

Under moderate temperature and humidity conditions, filler will be dry and ready to sand in 25 minutes.

If the humidity is high, curing takes longer. Allow at least 45 minutes. If it's hot and dry, the filler cures faster, sometimes in as little as 10 minutes.

Some body filler kits include a plastic filler spreader that is the same color as correctly mixed filler and hardener. By comparing the color of mixed filler with the color of the spreader, you can tell if you have the mixture correct, or need to add filler (mixture too dark) or hardener (mixture too light).

HOW TO APPLY BODY FILLER

Just as important as mixing is the technique you use to apply body filler. *Filler must be put on in thin layers and pressed firmly into the dent.* Again, keeping air bubbles out is important for a clean, smooth finish.

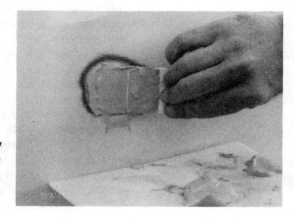

Apply a small dab of filler to the dent. Press firmly with the spreader, laying down a single, very thin first layer.

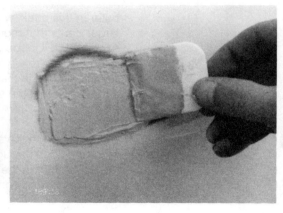

Apply additional thin coats of filler until the area is slightly higher than the surrounding painted surface. This usually requires about two or three layers of filler.

HOW TO SAND BODY FILLER

Sanding seems like such a simple and obvious thing to do. But that's why most people do it wrong.

The most common *wrong* way to sand is to fold the sandpaper in half and use your bare hand to rub the sandpaper around the surface. This creates an uneven surface because your fingers follow the bumps and waves in the filler. You make them smoother—but you don't make a *flat* surface.

To sand correctly, you *must* use a flexible rubber sanding block to hold the sandpaper. Most auto parts stores carry sanding blocks. You can also find them in home improvement, hardware, and paint stores. Don't waste your time and spoil your job by trying to sand without this tool.

Later in this book, when we're working on larger dents that require more filler and sanding, we'll introduce you to a "cheese grater." If you're working on a dent larger than about 3 inches in diameter, a cheese grater can be a great time saver. (See page 87 for an example.)

Pay attention to the sandpaper grits recommended throughout this book. Using the correct grit in the correct order makes the job go faster and contributes to quality results.

Begin sanding the filler with 80-grit sandpaper. *Work from the outside edges of the filled area to the center.*

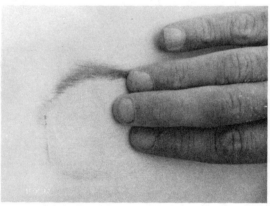

Check your progress often with your fingertips. *Continue sanding until the surface is consistently smooth to the touch. You'll need to sand a few inches of the surrounding paint to get a smooth transition.*

Continue sanding with 200-grit then 400-grit sandpaper. *When you sand, always start with the lower (more coarse) numbers, and work your way toward the higher (finer) numbers. Use the fine grades of sandpaper to produce a thin feathered edge on the filler.*

HOW TO TELL WHEN YOU'RE DONE SANDING

The goal in sanding a repair is to produce a smooth, flat surface that is level with the surrounding area. To know when you have reached this point, run your bare hand over the surface, and feel for high and low spots. Move your hand from the untouched painted surface through the sanded surface, and let your fingers "show" you what your eyes can't see. You will find that your light finger touch is the most accurate way to assess the surface.

After each sanding step, wipe the surface with a clean, dry rag. This ensures that your hand will feel only the surface and not any sanding residue.

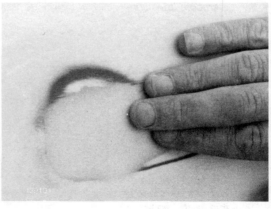

Check for a smooth, uniform surface. Run your hand from side to side, up and down, and then in a circular motion. Use a flexible steel ruler to verify high or low spots you can feel.

If you have a low spot, mix and apply another thin layer of filler. Repeat the sanding and filling process until the job is perfect.

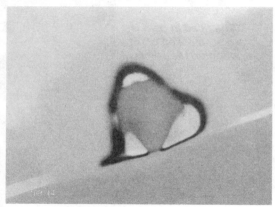

The finished job. A smooth, level patch with a good transition from paint to patch.

The surface of the repair must be smooth and level with the surrounding area for a first-class job. Be patient. Take the time to do a job you can be proud of.

FINISHING STEPS

NOTE: The following photos show you this job through its completion. However, very detailed instructions on how to mask, sand, primer, and paint are given in Section 10. (But we wanted you to see this project through to completion!)

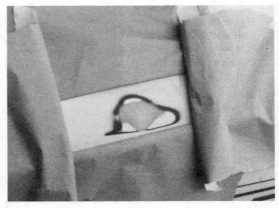

The filled in dent is masked off in preparation for primer.
See the Pro Tip: How to Mask Like A Pro on page 143.

Before priming, a tack cloth is used to clean the surface.

The repair area is then sprayed with primer *as detailed on page 150.*

The primer is sanded in preparation for final painting. *The edges are carefully feathered.*

Final paint is applied in very thin layers.

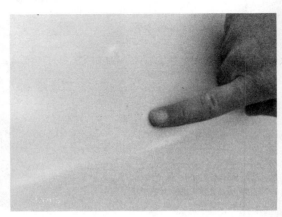

The finished job after the final paint has been rubbed with compound and waxed. You can't tell where the dent was! This is the payoff for careful work.

Section 5:
Professional Dent Pulling Techniques

If a dent is more than about 1/4-inch deep, it *must* be pulled out before filling. (See the *Pro Tip* on page 35 for how to measure dent depth.) Never just slather filler into a deep dent and sand it off. Thick filler will crack and fall out. It is actually quite easy to pull out dents—even if you've never done it before. Follow our instructions carefully, work slowly, and check your progress often.

We recommend that you use two basic types of pullers: a suction puller for large shallow dents with soft edges and a slide-hammer puller for others. We will show you how to use a T-handle puller on a small dent, but a slide-hammer puller is actually much easier to control.

Your goal in pulling a dent is not to restore the sheet metal perfectly to its original shape. (The professionals get amazingly close, however.) Your goal is to use the puller to bring the sheet metal back to approximately its original shape— but *never higher than it was originally.* This way you can use body filler to precisely match the original contours of the body panel.

TOOLS AND SUPPLIES

■ **Dent puller**—Either a suction-cup, T-handle, or slide-hammer puller, depending on the dent. These are very inexpensive tools and are essential for doing a proper job.

■ **Electric drill motor and drills**—Used to drill holes for either a T-handle or slide-hammer dent puller.

■ **Duct tape or masking tape**—Used as a guide to keep the drill from going too deep.

■ **Chalk, crayon, or marker pen**—For marking the holes to be drilled in the sheet metal.

■ **Steel ruler**—To check progress of dent pulling and verify that the sheet metal surface is flat.

■ **Body hammer**—Used to assist in the dent pulling process. A regular smooth-face hammer will also work.

You might also want to assemble the items listed on page 36 so that once you've pulled the dent, you can proceed with filling.

HOW TO USE A SUCTION-CUP PULLER

Dents that can be pulled out with a suction cup are fairly smooth, with no sharply creased corners. They often look like what you'd get if you were to press a football into sheet metal—no distinct lines, no sharp edges, just a gradual depression.

The perfect dent for a suction cup puller is an "oil-can" dent in a large, gently curved panel. With this type of damage, there is often no stretching of the metal or damage to the paint. Many oil-can dents need no further work than a pull with a suction cup. Typical oil-can dents are produced by forcing a door shut with your knee when your arms are full of grocery bags, or by a child playing on the hood or roof.

A suction-cup puller is the easiest puller to use. Usually made of rubber, suction cups are available in several sizes. The ones most commonly used are about the size of a saucer. You'll also need a garden hose or a bucket of water for wetting the body panel.

The dent in this roof is a perfect candidate for pulling with a suction cup. Dents that are easily handled with a suction cup include soft depression dents in trunks, hoods, roofs, and doors.

A sharp-edged compression dent, like this one, can't be fixed with a suction cup. It's best dealt with by using a slide-hammer dent puller.

Wet the compression dent, and press the suction cup firmly and evenly into it. Push the air out of the cup to create a suction between the cup and the dent.

Now pull—slowly! It's easy to overpull a dent and create a raised bump in the panel. Remember— the sheet metal has already been "tortured" and stretched once. Be gentle!

If the suction cup doesn't have a release button, push the cup to one side. This will break the seal and release the cup.

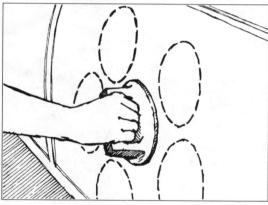

Suction cups should be used progressively over an area. Don't attempt to pull the dent out all at once. Instead, move the suction cup around, pulling different parts of the dent, until you have pulled it back to the original shape.

HOW TO USE A T-HANDLE DENT PULLER ON A SMALL DENT

A T-handle puller can be used to move the metal back into position on a variety of small dents. In addition to the puller, you will need a drill motor and a small drill bit—slightly larger than the diameter of the puller hook.

The goal is to pull the dent so that it can be filled with less than a 1/4-inch thickness of plastic body filler.

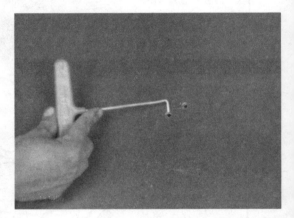

To use a T-Handle puller, first drill one or two small holes in the center of the dent. Insert the hook tip of the puller into a hole.

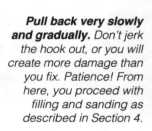

Pull back very slowly and gradually. Don't jerk the hook out, or you will create more damage than you fix. Patience! From here, you proceed with filling and sanding as described in Section 4.

HOW TO MAP AND DRILL A DENT FOR SLIDE-HAMMER PULLING

Before you can effectively pull out a dent, you must "map" or mark it to determine where pulling force is required. This means simply locating the lowest points and deciding how to bring them up to the level of the original surface. Spending a few minutes mapping and planning will help you to control the movement of the metal for an easier job with professional results.

A typical dent that requires pulling. It is more than 1/4-inch deep and has some sharp creases at the edge.

Analyze the dent with your fingertips. Find the point of impact, usually the deepest part of the dent.

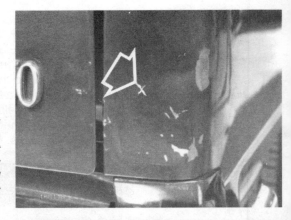

Begin mapping the dent.
Use chalk for dark
colored cars, or a felt tip
pen for light colors. Start
with a mark in the deepest
portion of the dent, and
mark pulling points about
an inch apart.

**Once the dent is
completely mapped,**
you'll have a line of marks
that starts in the center of
the dent, up to within
1/2-inch of the uninjured
sheet metal.

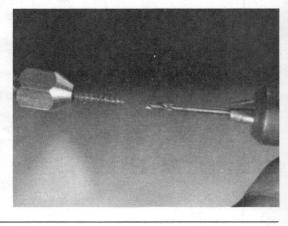

**Select a drill bit that's
smaller than the sheet
metal screw in the
puller.** In many cases a
9/64-inch bit is the one
you need. Compare the
end of your dent puller
with your drill bit to be
sure you're using the
right one. If in doubt,
start small.

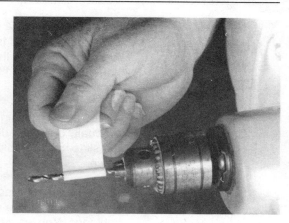

Wrap tape 1/2-inch from the tip of the drill, and drill all the spots you've marked. The tape serves as a stop to prevent you from drilling too deeply into the panel and damaging upholstery or wiring.

HOW TO USE A SLIDE-HAMMER DENT PULLER

A word of caution: A dent puller is a powerful tool. Start easy and take your time. Don't try to pull out a dent with just the very first hole—or the very first "whack" from the slide hammer.

A dent puller is designed to gently and gradually pull out a dent. Use easy hits with the slide hammer to coax the metal back into place.

As the metal approaches its original shape, decrease your force on the slide hammer to light taps. You want to avoid forcing the metal out too far, creating bumps and ridges that then have to be knocked back down.

Again, the goal is to bring the sheet metal back into its original position, so that less than a 1/4-inch coat of body filler is needed.

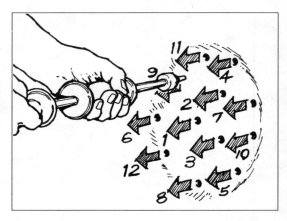

Pull the dent back into shape with several progressive easy passes. *Generally, work from the deepest part of the dent to the shallowest. Don't try to force the metal. Details are shown on the following pages.*

Insert the dent puller tip into the hole at the deepest point in the dent. *After the screw gets a bite, turn it **only** one-half turn more.*

Hold the handle of the dent puller in one hand. *You pound with the slide weight in your other.*

To pull, slide the weight quickly from the bottom to the top of the handle. *It should hit the handle with a solid clunk. Tap several times, until the metal moves slightly, then move on to the next hole.*

Always keep the dent puller 90 degrees to the surface. *When the puller is held at an angle, as shown here, the dent will be pulled in the direction of the puller, rather than straight out.*

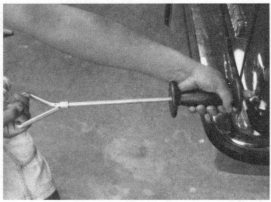

You'll probably pull on four or five holes before you see much response from the sheet metal. *Remember, it's better to go around a few times and work slowly than to try to do it all at once and pull the sheet metal out too far.*

After you've made a couple of passes around the entire dent, *check your progress with a steel ruler. It will help you see high and low spots. Bring up low spots with light taps of the puller.*

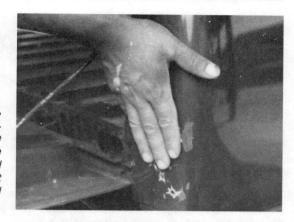

As you near completion, don't rely on your eyes. Run your hand across the surface to determine areas that still need pulling and those that are okay. Be careful of sharp edges.

In some cases a little assistance from a sheet metal hammer is necessary. Here, we're straightening the edge while pulling on the main dent.

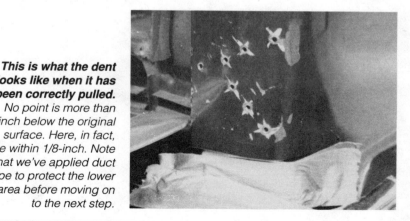

This is what the dent looks like when it has been correctly pulled. No point is more than 1/4-inch below the original surface. Here, in fact, we're within 1/8-inch. Note that we've applied duct tape to protect the lower area before moving on to the next step.

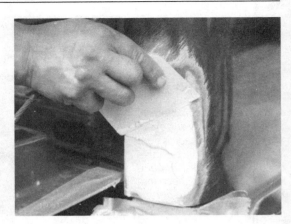

Only a thin coat of filler is now needed. The puller holes are filled with the body filler. Final shaping and sanding is done as described in Section 4. Painting is described in Section 10.

Section 6:
A Larger Dent Pulling Project

INTRODUCTION

Even though a large dent may look intimidating, it is really no more difficult to fix than the small one we showed you in the previous section. You will still use the basic techniques of mapping, slide-hammer pulling, filling, and painting.

In this section, we're going to take you in detail through a larger project: a double hit on the side of a full-size pickup truck. We assume you've read the preceding sections on dent filling and slide-hammer technique.

Here you'll see how those techniques work on a much larger project, and you'll learn more about how to apply them to your own repair.

TOOLS AND SUPPLIES

- **Electric drill and bits**—For drilling holes for the dent puller and for sanding off paint to bare metal.

- **Steel ruler and quarter**—To measure the progress of your dent repair.

- **Slide-hammer dent puller**—For raising sheet metal and reducing depth of dent.

- **Sheet metal hammer**—For shaping the sheet metal surface during pulling.

- **Masking tape and masking paper**—For protecting surrounding areas.

- **Circular sanding disc and matching-size sandpaper discs (40-, 80-, and 150-grit)**—For sanding paint off to prepare for body filler.

- **Wax-and-silicone remover or lacquer thinner**—To prepare surface for body filler.

- **Plastic body filler and hardener**—For filling in shallow dent to perfect surface.

- **Filler mixing board and applicator**—For mixing and applying body filler.

- **Cheese grater**—To remove excess filler.

- **Flexible rubber sanding block and sandpaper (40-, 80-, 200-,400-, 600-, and 1000-grit)**—To sand filler, primer, and paint.

- **Glazing and spot putty**—For filling minor imperfections.

- **Aerosol automotive primer**— For preparing repaired area for finish painting.

- **Aerosol automotive paint**—Color must match (page 4). Clear-coat, if needed.

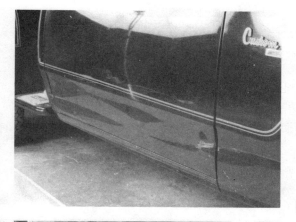

BEFORE:
Our project vehicle. Note how the dent involves three body panels: the fender behind the wheel well, the door and the cab. Nice shot!

AFTER:
Project vehicle plus about 6 hours of do-it-yourself work. *All the panels have been pulled and filled. The door edge required straightening. Using just inexpensive do-it-yourself equipment and aerosol primer and paint, the results are up to professional standards. Total savings: over $300!*

As you consider your own repair project, remember the one big advantage you have over the professional: you can take the time necessary to do the job right. He has to contend with a flat-rate repair manual. Don't hurry your work.

Study our instructions and plan your own job carefully. Always know where you're going, and check each step in your progress to obtain top quality results.

MAPPING AND PULLING

The first step in any repair is to measure the dent. *Use your steel ruler and quarter to measure the low spot. This dent is more than 1/4-inch deep and will require pulling.*

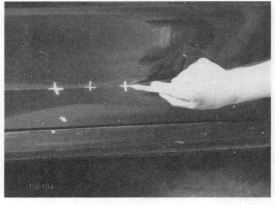

Begin mapping out the dent in the lowest, deepest section of the dent. *Use a crayon or felt-tip marker.*

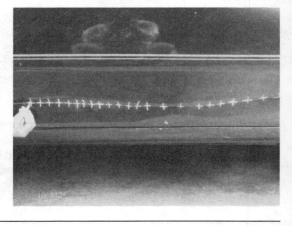

Work out from the lowest spot, marking a planned pulling hole about every inch or so.

Here, the entire dent has been mapped. *The cross marks follow the deepest portions of the dent and show you where to drill holes for the puller.*

Drill a hole for the puller at each cross point. *Be sure to select the correct drill bit size and wrap it with tape as described on page 61.*

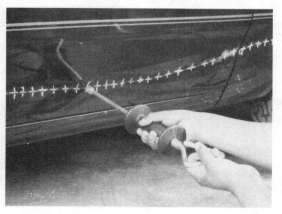

Starting at the lowest spot on the dent, begin the pulling process. *Pull moderately; the process may require several passes. (See page 62 for details on how to use a slide-hammer puller.)*

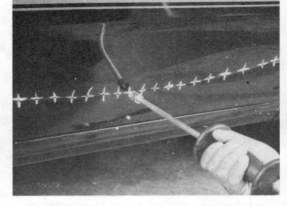

Continue pulling at each successive hole. *Be patient, and don't try to do the whole job in just one pass.*

If you accidentally pull the metal out too far, hammer it back in. *A few taps with a sheet metal hammer will push the metal back into place.*

Here is our progress, *as we work toward the front of the door.*

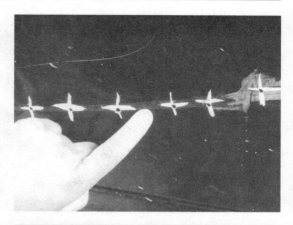

A fairly common situation when you use a dent puller is to discover some small areas between holes that haven't come up to the same level as the surrounding area.

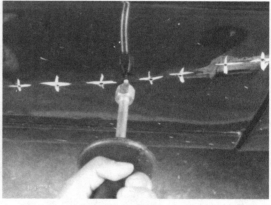

The fix: drill an additional hole and pull this surface up to the desired level. You can always drill more holes wherever you need them.

Once again, our pulling accidentally brought the surface too high. So we used the hammer to tap it back down.

Hammering was also needed at the edge of the door, where the sheet metal folds under. When we pulled out the center of the dent, the edges came out too far, so we hammered them back into position. You do whatever is needed to get the results you want.

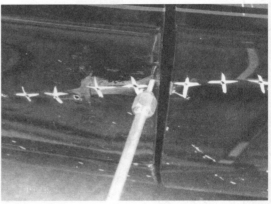

An additional pulling hole was needed right at the door edge. Take the time to make sure that door edges are as close to their original position as possible. You don't want a lot of filler here, which would make the edge of the door look thick and the repair obvious.

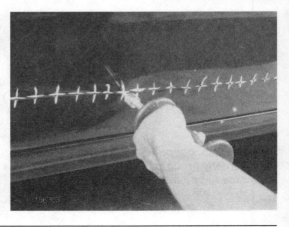

Switching over to the left side of the door panel, the dent pulling process continues.

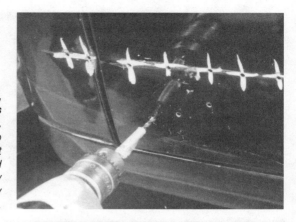

As you pull the dent, you will run across "snags" in the process. *The dent pulled up correctly, but an adjacent area is still "bound" and buckled. Simply drill a few more holes in the newly developed depression...*

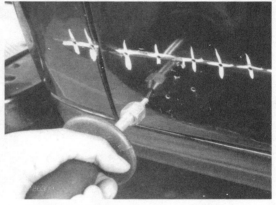

...and pull adjacent areas just like the main dent. *Only a few taps on the slide puller were required to pop this back into position.*

Another low spot is discovered and drilled. *Keep checking the contour as you go.*

When pulling this dent, adjacent metal started to come out too far. *To correct it, we tapped the metal in while applying steady tension on the puller.*

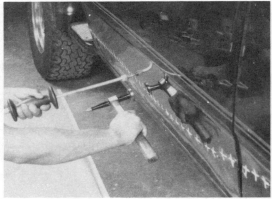

We keep pulling and hammering until the door is complete. *We rethreaded the dent puller into holes that came up too high. We then applied light pulling tension while tapping the metal back down into the desired position.*

The small dent in the cab pulled normally.

But the door jamb has a small bow that requires hammering back into position. The trick is to keep pulling tension on the hole as you tap the bulge down.

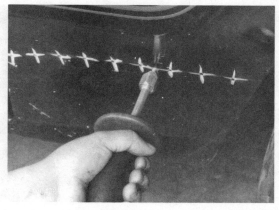

Moving up front to the fender panel, the dent puller is effective in bringing the sheet metal back near its original position.

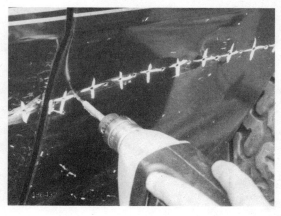

But once again, we discovered a depressed area that required additional drilling and pulling—a normal occurrence. The point is simple: drill and pull wherever needed to get the desired end result!

In some cases, when you're almost done, a new problem spot will appear. This time it was near the door. Drilling, pulling, and hammering brought it into line. Check over your whole job, and fine-tune any problem spots you find.

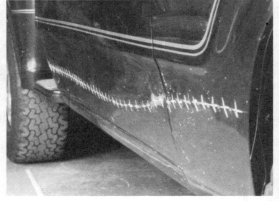

Pulling completed! All three panels are back very close to their original position. We've checked to make sure that nothing is higher than the original surface and nothing is more than 1/4 inch below it. (Actually, nothing here is more than 1/8-inch deep.) Compare this to where we started, on page 69.

APPLYING BODY FILLER

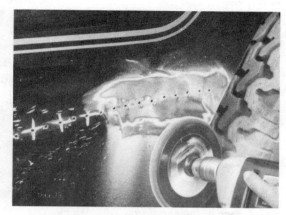

Prepare the surface by sanding away all paint to bare metal. *Use a 40-grit disc on your electric drill. Remove the paint from the damaged surface plus about 2 inches around it.*

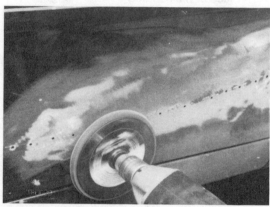

Here's our progress in sanding off the paint about half way through the job. *Notice that we are sanding to bare metal about 2 inches above and below the dent. It is essential that you reach bare metal on all places that will receive filler. It will not adhere properly to a painted surface.*

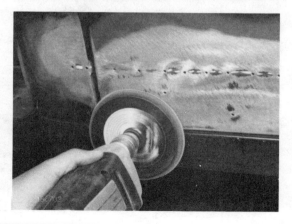

Here, we are finishing our sanding of the entire repair area. *Notice how the edges are nicely feathered and smooth. As you sand, be careful not to create a ridged or uneven surface that will show through your final paint.*

PRO TIP: How to Use a Disc Sander

Using your electric drill with a sanding disc can be a time saver for removing paint to bare metal. Here's how to get good results.

Never put the entire face of the sanding disc on the surface you're sanding! *The disc is hard to control in this position and the results will be very inconsistent.*

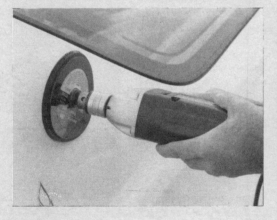

Don't use the bottom edge of the sanding disc. *You can't see your work well, and you will not have good, precise control.*

This is the correct angle and attitude, sanding with the top edge of the disc. Use only the outer inch or so, and hold the drill motor at an angle slightly higher than the area you are sanding.

Remember: use a sanding disc *only* for removing paint—never for shaping body filler. Body filler requires much more precision to match contours and avoid gouges.

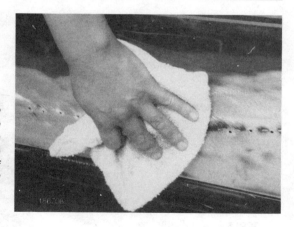

When you're done sanding, wipe down the entire area with wax-and-silicone remover. This get rid of the tiny metal, paint, and sandpaper particles that you can't see.

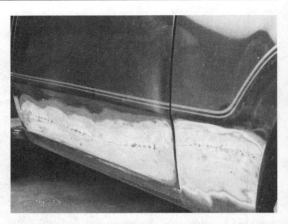

Ready for filler? The dent has been pulled, paint sanded down, and residue wiped off. But before you begin applying filler...

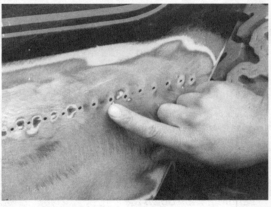

...check the surface again with your fingers. It's normal to find a few high spots or low spots. Be careful of sharp hole edges.

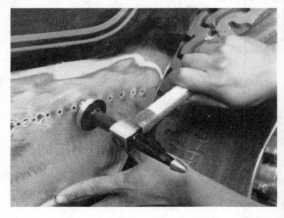

Tap down the high spots, and pull any low spots. With the metal now bare, you can make any final corrections before proceeding. Remember, no spot can be higher than the original body contour. Low spots can still be filled.

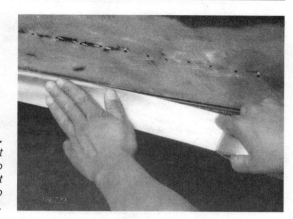

Protect adjacent areas. Here, the door sill didn't need any body filler, so we put a layer of stout duct tape over it to protect it from damage.

Prepare the body filler by stirring the can thoroughly. Use a stick to mix all the ingredients that settle to the bottom.

Ladle out enough body filler on your mixing board to do one thin layer over the repair. Don't put more on the mixing board than you can apply in about 5 minutes. With a repair as large as this one, we knew it would take several batches.

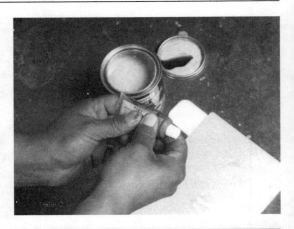

Prepare the tube of hardener by "working" it in the tube. *Squeeze it from one end to the other for at least a minute to make sure its ingredients are thoroughly mixed.*

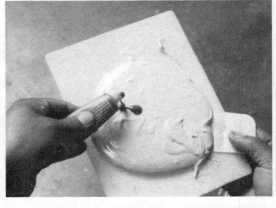

Squeeze a small amount of hardener onto the filler. *A dab about the size of a dime is all that was needed here. The more hardener you use, the faster the filler will set.*

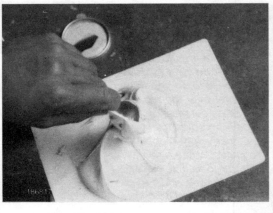

Mix the filler and hardener with a circular motion. *Press the mixture down from time to time to get out any air bubbles. Stir in both directions.*

Continue mixing for a minute or two—until the hardener is thoroughly mixed into the filler. *Look for a consistent color, with no swirl marks. Work quickly now—get the filler applied in the next 5 minutes or so.*

Put a small amount of filler on your applicator.

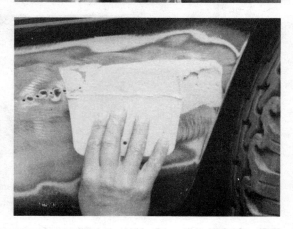

Apply a thin coat of body filler in an up-and-down motion. *Use moderate pressure to work the filler well into the metal and the pulling holes.*

Then, smooth this first layer right-to-left to make sure it's thin and even. *Feather the filler at the edges. Your goal is to lay down a good base for subsequent sanding and shaping.*

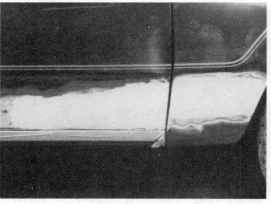

Here's where we ran out of our first batch of body filler. *We're about half way through the door. No problem. We just mixed another batch and continued on.*

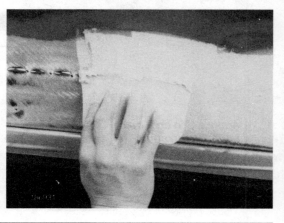

Continue filling the repair area until the entire surface is covered with body filler.

SHAPING AND SANDING

With the body filler still slightly soft, rough shape it with a "cheese grater" file. *Wait a few minutes until the filler becomes firm, but is still pliable—like cheese! Shaping now saves sanding time later.*

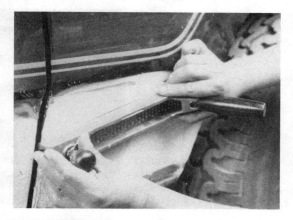

Check for low spots and, if necessary, fill them. *Mix another batch of filler and hardener, and apply it where needed.*

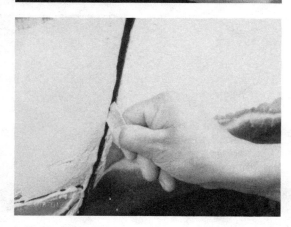

Use a razor blade to clean excess filler from the edge of body panels. *It's easier to remove before it's fully hardened.*

When the filler has hardened, shape it to the original body contours with 40-grit sandpaper. *You must use a flexible sanding block. Don't feather the edges too thin with this coarse sandpaper.*

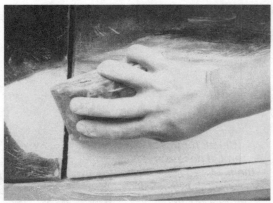

Switch to a 150-grit sandpaper, and continue with final shaping. *Look for high spots, and remove them. Now you can feather the edges of the filler so that the surface is totally smooth.*

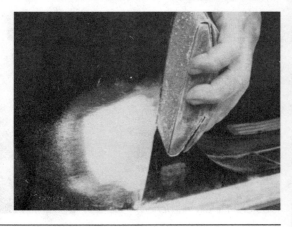

Be sure to open the doors, and shape the edges and corners. *You want the door jams and door edges to look as nice and finished as the body itself.*

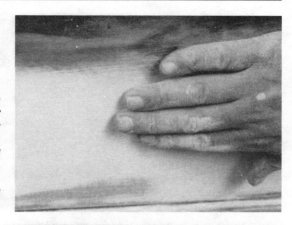

Frequently wipe off the dust, and check your sanding progress. *Your hand will reveal high spots, low spots, and ridges that your eyes cannot see. Rub both up and down and from side to side.*

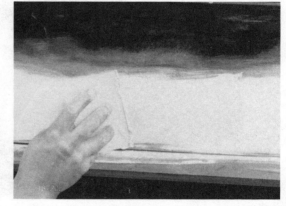

Whoops! After checking this area, we had to fix a few "waves" in the surface. *More body filler was mixed and a thin coat applied.*

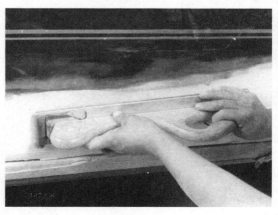

A long sanding board can produce a nice flat surface on longer body panels. *We used an inexpensive commercial board, but you could even improvise one with 2-by-4 lumber.*

Continue the sanding, checking, and filling process until the surface is perfect. The nice thing about do-it-yourself body work with plastic filler is that you can easily recover from mistakes. If you sand too much, put on another layer of filler and try again.

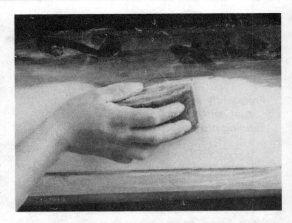

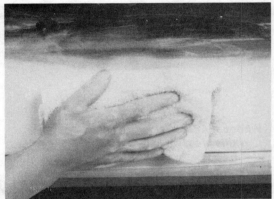

When you're completely satisfied with the repair area, wipe it clean with a dry rag.

SURFACE PRIMING

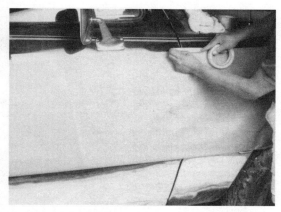

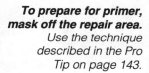

To prepare for primer, mask off the repair area. *Use the technique described in the Pro Tip on page 143.*

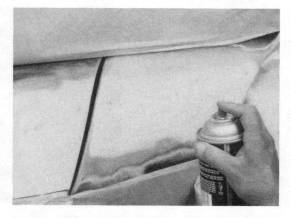

Apply a thin first coat of primer. *If done right, you'll be able to see through it. You don't want a thick heavy coat, which can sag and drip. Don't forget to shake the aerosol can thoroughly before using it.*

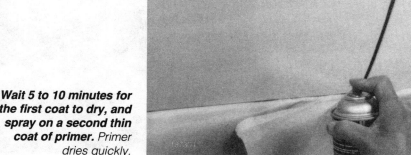

Wait 5 to 10 minutes for the first coat to dry, and spray on a second thin coat of primer. *Primer dries quickly.*

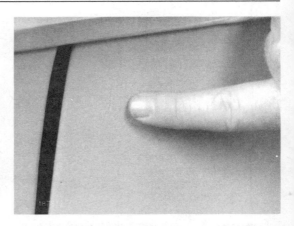

Inspect the surface very closely to locate imperfections. *Primer gives you a great preview of the finished surface. It is totally normal to find small pinholes and "cat claw" marks at this stage. We found several on our job here.*

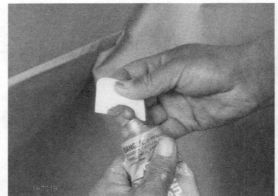

Put glaze and spot putty on a small applicator.

Apply a very thin coat to every imperfection you locate. *Use your flexible applicator to press it into the offending spots.*

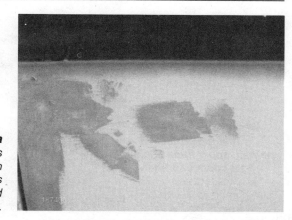

Our job had more than a few "hickies" to fill. *This is normal. Inspect with your hand and eyes very closely, and get them all now.*

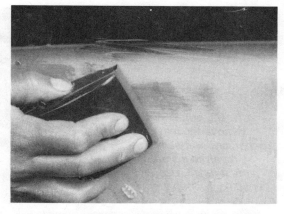

After the spot putty has dried (about 15 minutes), wet-sand with 400- or 600-grit sandpaper. *Simply dip the sanding block and paper in a bucket of water and go for it. Most of the putty will be sanded away, with extremely fine feathered edges.*

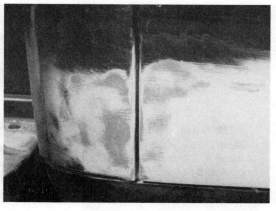

Sand the putty until the surface is perfect. *Again, use your hand to check for a perfect transition from filler to putty. The contrasting color of the putty here shows where paper-thin areas have been filled with it. This surface is glossy smooth.*

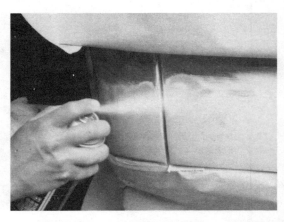

When you're satisfied that the surface is perfect, apply three final light coats of primer. *Allow the first two coats to dry before applying the third.*

After the primer dries, remove the masking paper, and wet-sand the repair to a smooth, perfect finish. *Use 400- or 600-grit sandpaper on your sanding block.*

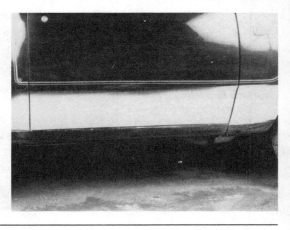

The finished primer stage. *Check your work again to make sure it's smooth and perfect. Final paint will not hide any surface imperfections.*

FINAL FINISH

Mask the repair area again, using the technique shown in the Pro Tip on page 143. Note how we've used plastic garbage bags to protect the wheels from paint overspray.

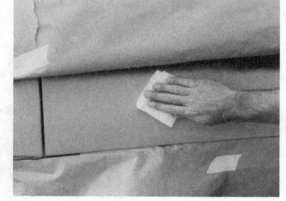

Clean the surface thoroughly with a tack cloth. This removes any dust.

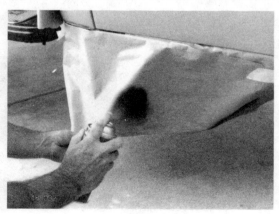

Shake the aerosol can well, and test the pattern on your masking paper. You want to make sure the paint is properly mixed and your distance is about right. If you're too close, the paint will run; too far, it will blow away. Usually, 8 to 12 inches is about right.

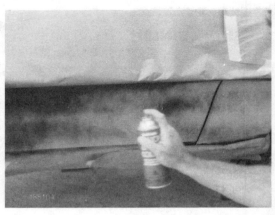

Apply a very thin first coat of paint. *It will probably look sort of spotted. That's okay. Let the first coat dry for at least 15 minutes.*

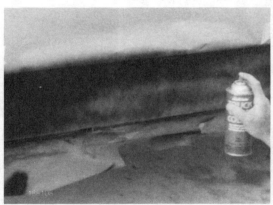

Apply a very thin second coat of color paint. *Don't worry about covering the primer yet. This coat will probably still look somewhat spotty from the droplets of paint. Allow it to dry for at least 15 minutes.*

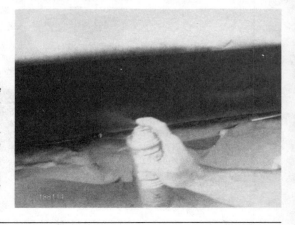

Apply a thin third coat of color paint. *Now, you'll see the body color fill in quite nicely. And by painting with several thin coats rather than one thick coat, you won't have runs and sags in your finish.*

Apply one or several more thin coats of color, until the coverage is complete. *Allow at least 15 minutes between each coat. (If you are matching a clear-coat finish, you would spray clear after the color coverage is complete.) Do not apply a "wet" coat to produce a shinier finish. The shine is brought up later with polishing compound.*

The finished paint needs to cure for at least a week before polishing and waxing. *But even here you can see the high quality professional results. And remember, this was all done with a few inexpensive tools and aerosol paint!*

This job was finished with polishing compound and wax to bring up the sheen of the paint to match the surrounding area. For a full description of painting procedures, see Section 10.

Good Advice:

The most common problems and mistakes made in touch-ups and repairs are the result of rushing the job. One body and paint expert explains it this way:

"If you can't find the time to do it right, you'll always find yourself doing it over. I quit trying to shave off 10 minutes when I realized that each time I did, it cost me two more hours."

Section 7:

Hammer and Dolly Techniques

Most of the dents an amateur should attack are best handled with a slide-hammer puller. If, however, you want to build your body-repair skills, you will want to begin experimenting with hammering out dents. This requires practice.

The purpose of this section is to get you off to a good start by introducing you to the two basic techniques used by professionals: the hammer-on-dolly method and the hammer-off-dolly method. These methods require access to *both sides* of a body panel. The following pages give you basic how-to information to get you started. We recommend that you practice on salvage body panels before the real thing.

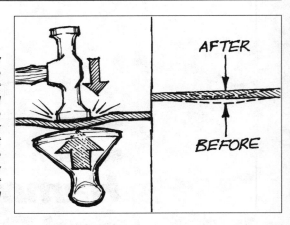

__The hammer-on-dolly method__ is used to raise sheet metal and bring it back to its original contour. Although the hammer strikes the outer surface of the sheet metal, it's steady pressure from the heavy dolly behind the metal that pushes the metal out and back into shape.

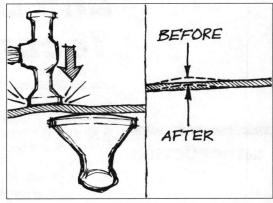

__In the hammer-off-dolly method,__ the hammer knocks the sheet metal down while the dolly supports adjacent metal to prevent it from being knocked down also.

Hammer-and-dolly work begins in a big way, as you quickly move sheet metal back into position. As work progresses, you fine-tune the repair with your finishing hammer to take out tiny bumps and dimples. You will probably need to finish your repairs with a thin layer of body filler for an absolutely smooth finish. But skilled pros can often hammer metal perfectly back to its original shape!

It's easy to over-hammer a dent. Too many blows to a piece of sheet metal will stretch it—a condition that's difficult to correct for anyone other than an experienced pro. As we've stressed throughout this book, *patience* is the key to good body work. Take it easy with the hammer and dolly, and you'll get good results. Go too fast, and you'll torture the sheet metal beyond salvation!

TOOLS AND EQUIPMENT

■ **Sheet metal hammers**—Special hammers designed for sheet metal work.

■ **Dollies**—Hand-held metal "anvils" used in conjunction with sheet metal hammers.

■ **A scrap fender**—Optional, but a great way to practice pounding technique before working on your own vehicle.

PLANNING YOUR APPROACH

As with dent pulling, you should plan your hammer and dolly work, although it's not necessary to actually mark the sheet metal.

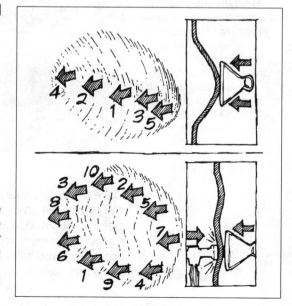

The work sequence is important. Start in the lowest areas, gradually working your way to the outer edge of the dent, using a criss-cross pattern as shown.

HOW TO HAMMER-ON-DOLLY

The hammer-on-dolly method is used to bring dented sheet metal back up to the level of the surrounding panel. With this method, the dolly does most of the work moving the metal back into shape.

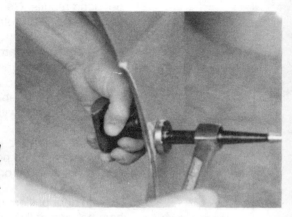

Hold the dolly behind the dent, on the low side of the sheet metal, where you plan to hit it with your hammer.

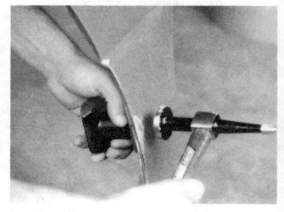

Hold the dolly against the metal with firm, even pressure. Remember— the dolly is moving the metal and must remain in contact with it. Don't allow it to bounce back. The hammer should bounce off the surface each time you hit it. And you should hear a ring that signals you are hitting the spot supported by the dolly.

Move the dolly about an inch after each hit and repeat the process to bring the sheet metal back out. Gradually raise the dent until it's level with the surrounding metal. Be accurate. If you miss the dolly, you'll probably add a new dent to the sheet metal.

HOW TO HAMMER-OFF-DOLLY

The hammer-off-dolly method is used to push in sheet metal from the surrounding surface. Use this method to knock down any high spots you might accidentally create by hammering or pulling out a dent too far.

With this technique, the hammer does most of the work as it knocks down the high spots next to the dolly. If you were to hammer without the dolly, the high spot would still go down, but it would also lower the height of surrounding sheet metal.

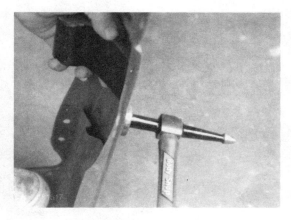

In hammer-off-dolly situations, hammer blows should be a series of light blows. *Each hit is much softer than the hammer-on-dolly technique.*

Since you can't see the dolly, tap lightly around the general area with the hammer until you locate the dolly. Listen for the change in sound. Tap only on areas that are raised above the normal level of the sheet metal. Never hit a spot that's level with or lower than the surrounding bodywork.

HOW TO PERFORM FINE HAMMERING

We've shown you two basic hammer-and-dolly techniques. Fine hammering is nothing more than using those same two techniques but with lighter blows of a small "pick" head for finer shaping.

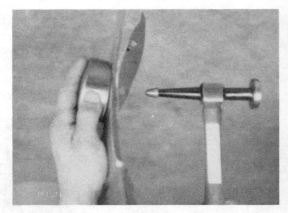

Use the "pick" head for fine hammering work on *small peaks and dimples.*

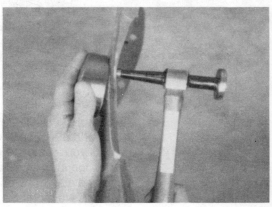

Fine hammering isn't really hammering. It's *more like "tapping." Numerous, light taps are the key. Hold the hammer at about mid-handle to reduce your leverage.*

As you practice hammer-and-dolly techniques, you'll see how they work to restore damaged sheet metal to its original shape. After you've gained some experience, you'll be ready to tackle a few dents on your own car or truck.

Section 8:

How to Repair Cracks in Fiberglass and ABS

INTRODUCTION

Okay, so you don't own a Corvette. But if your car or truck was built in the last 20 years, there is a high probability that it has some fiberglass or ABS plastic body parts, particularly around the front and rear bumpers. Cracks in either fiberglass or ABS can be fixed with an inexpensive fiberglass-cloth patch kit.

Fiberglass and ABS plastic are different to work with than sheet metal. But the work requires the same attitude as sheet metal work: *Patience.*

Do be careful to follow the special precautions given on page 107 to protect your eyes, skin, and lungs.

Touch-Up & Dent Repair

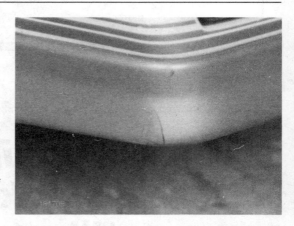

BEFORE:
*A typical problem—
getting too cozy with a
parking-lot concrete
curb.* This ABS plastic
body part is typical of
those found on millions
of cars today.

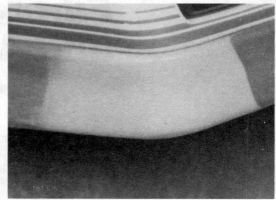

AFTER:
A perfect repair. This
was a simple job for a
do-it-yourselfer and saved
several hundred dollars!

PRO TIP: How to Prepare Yourself for Working With Fiberglass

WARNING: Fiberglass can be very harmful to your body. You must observe the following basic precautions when working with it.

Cover your skin. The materials in fiberglass, like polyester resin, can irritate your skin. Keep your arms covered with protective cream. (A long sleeve shirt is also a good idea.) Protective skin creams for working with fiberglass are available where fiberglass is sold. Apply a coat to your hands and arms, let it dry, and put on a second coat. Then rinse your arms under cold water to "set" the cream.

Protect your hands. Gloves are a must when working with fiberglass. Rubber surgical gloves work best. Many auto parts stores and drug stores carry them. If you do get material on your hands or arms, use lacquer thinner or soap and water to remove it before it dries and sets!

Protect your lungs. A mask is a must, especially when you're sanding or applying resin. A protective mask helps keep polyester fibers from entering your lungs.

Keep an eye on safety. Plastic safety glasses are essential when sanding. Getting fiberglass in your eyes is a painful experience. Sunglasses or regular prescription glasses won't do the job.

Watch the watchers. Fiberglass body work doesn't usually draw huge crowds, but the curious will often watch you close at hand. Make sure they understand the dangers and stay well away from the work.

After work clean-up. Always vacuum up all residue from your fiberglass work, and put away leftover materials. Fiberglass cloth and resin are of great interest to kids and pets. If these materials are accidentally swallowed, dilute stomach contents with milk and call a doctor immediately.

TOOLS AND SUPPLIES

- **Protective cream**—Used to protect your hands and arms.

- **Rubber gloves**—Worn when working with resin and hardener.

- **Dust mask**—Worn when mixing and sanding fiberglass.

- **Plastic safety glasses**—Worn when sanding fiberglass.

- **40-, 80-, 200-, and 400-grit sandpaper**—Used to rough up and prepare the surface for painting.

- **Fiberglass patch kit (contains fiberglass cloth, resin, and hardener)**—For repairing cracks in ABS plastic body parts as well as fiberglass.

- **Mixing sticks (ice cream sticks)**—Used to mix resin and hardener.

- **Scissors**—For cutting fiberglass cloth.

- **Small paintbrush**—For applying and removing resin.

- **Wax-and-silicone remover**—Prepares the surface so that fiberglass patches can adhere properly.

PRO TIP: How to Stop Cracks in Progress

If left unrepaired, a crack in fiberglass or ABS plastic will continue to grow. To keep it from growing until you can repair it, you should "stop-drill" the crack.

To stop a crack from spreading, look closely and find both ends of it. Then drill a 1/8-inch hole at the beginning and end of the crack.

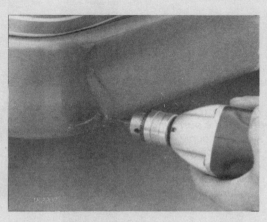

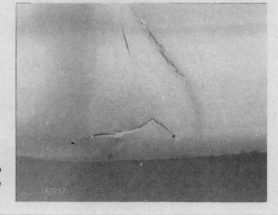

The holes relieve the pressure and stop the crack's progress.

HOW TO PREPARE THE SURFACE

The first step to a good fiberglass repair job is correct and careful preparation of the surface before you start. The surface area must be roughed up for the fiberglass patch to adhere well.

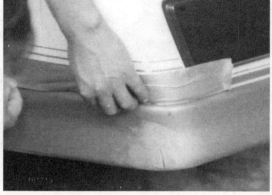

Before you begin work, protect the surrounding areas. A couple of layers of masking tape or duct tape will help protect the surrounding paint from scratches as you work.

Use 40-grit sandpaper to remove all the paint surrounding the crack. Prepare an area of several inches around the crack.

You must also sand on both edges of the crack. *You'll have to pull the two sides of the crack apart to gain access.*

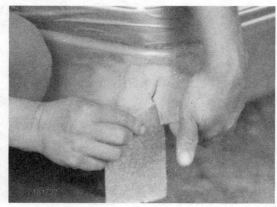

Slide the sandpaper into the crack and sand. *You must create a "V" shaped crack so the fiberglass patch has a good surface for bonding.*

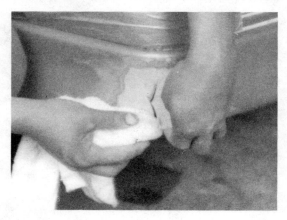

Clean the surface *and the surrounding area with wax-and-silicone remover.*

HOW TO PREPARE THE FIBERGLASS PATCH

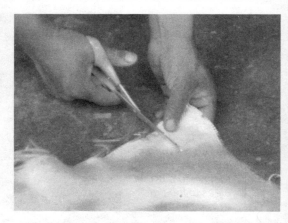

Cut a strip of fiberglass cloth that's slightly wider and longer than the crack. Cut the strip to follow the crack contour.

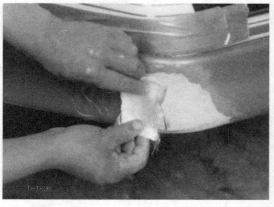

Set the cloth over the crack to make sure it covers the repair area. If the patch is much larger than the crack, it will result in a sloppy repair.

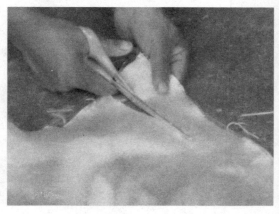

Cut two more strips of cloth. Each should extend at least 2 inches past the original patch. You will probably discover that it is necessary to sand away more paint to accommodate these patches.

HOW TO MIX RESIN

Pour a small amount of resin into a disposable mixing container. Use enough to saturate the fiberglass cloth patches.

Add a few drops of hardener in accordance with the directions in the kit. This hardener causes a chemical reaction that immediately starts hardening the resin. Follow the instructions carefully.

Mix the hardener thoroughly with a wooden stick. Thorough mixing helps eliminate pinholes in the finished job. You can tell it's done when it reaches a dark green color, and has a syrup-like consistency. Work quickly now, since the resin is beginning to harden.

HOW TO APPLY THE PATCH

Use a small brush to spread a thin layer of resin onto the crack area. *Spread it slightly larger than the first (smaller) fiberglass cloth patch. Note that you should wear rubber gloves to protect your hands.*

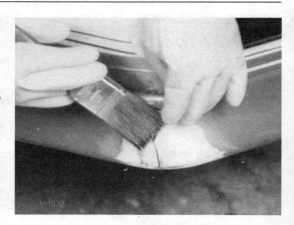

Dip the first (smaller) fiberglass cloth patch into the resin. *Get it thoroughly saturated.*

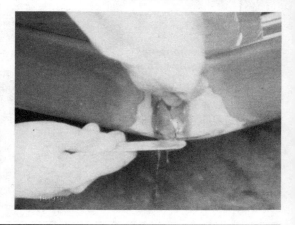

Apply the first (smaller) patch to the repair area. *Make sure it's flat and the edges aren't folded over. Brush more resin over the cloth to prepare for the next layers.*

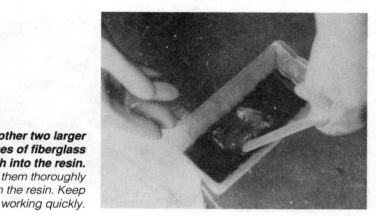

Dip the other two larger pieces of fiberglass cloth into the resin. *Saturate them thoroughly in the resin. Keep working quickly.*

Apply the other two larger pieces of cloth to the crack, one over the other. *Remove excess resin if possible, but don't be too concerned, because at this point, things will be getting very messy!*

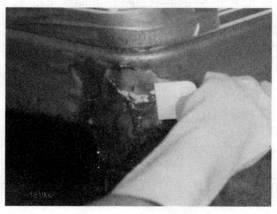

Use a plastic body filler applicator to spread the resin around as it begins to set up. *Don't worry about resin dripping down—it will be removed after it hardens.*

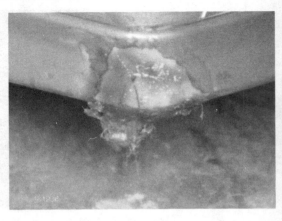

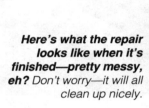

Here's what the repair looks like when it's finished—pretty messy, eh? Don't worry—it will all clean up nicely.

Now comes the really difficult part—waiting for the fiberglass to cure completely. The *Pro Tip* below gives you some idea of how long you will have to wait.

PRO TIP: Fiberglass Curing Times

The best time to perform fiberglass work is on warm, sunny days. Fiberglass cures best in direct sunlight. If you can't work outside, or the temperature is below 50°F (10°C), you'll need a sunlamp set about 6 inches from the patch to cure the resin. A hand-held hair dryer will also work. But don't be fooled by high temperatures—heat alone doesn't cure fiberglass. It takes time too.

Temperature	Sunny	Partly Cloudy
90°F (32°C)	0.5 to 1 hour	1 to 3 hours
75°F (24°C)	1 to 1.5 hours	2 to 6 hours
50°F (10°C)	3 to 10 hours	8 to 24 hours

Once the fiberglass has completely cured and is very hard, you can prepare it for primer and painting.

HOW TO FINISH THE FIBERGLASS PATCH

Use scissors or snips to cut off the excess cloth and resin *below the repair area.*

Sand the area with rough 40-grit sandpaper *to take down the high spots. Sanding fiberglass is similar to sanding body filler. It just takes longer because the material is harder.*

Repeat the sanding process in two more steps, first with 120-grit sandpaper and then with 200-grit. *This is where you will match the original body contours. If you are sanding a flat panel, be sure to use a sanding block.*

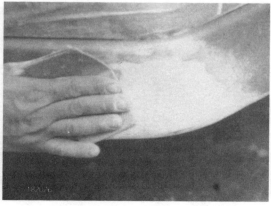

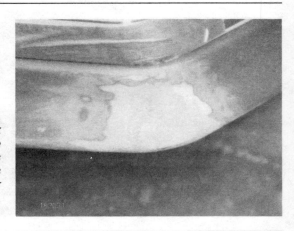

When finished sanding, the repair should look something like this. *Note the nice feathered edges of the patches. This feels very smooth, except for a few small pinholes, which are normal.*

Mask off the lower portion of the repair, and mix a new batch of resin and hardener to fill the pinholes. *You can use epoxy solder, but many pros prefer resin because it's harder.*

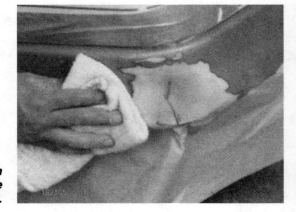

Clean the area with wax-and-silicone remover.

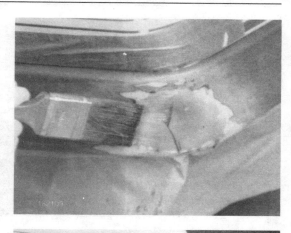

Using a paint brush, apply a very thin layer of the resin-and-hardener over the patched area. Brush out any air bubbles, and then let it cure until fully hardened.

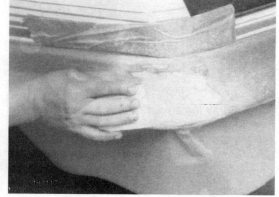

Once the area has cured fully, sand it with 80-grit sandpaper, followed by 200-grit, and finally 400-grit.

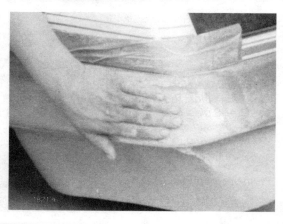

Continue sanding and checking the repair with your hands. When the repair is absolutely smooth, stop sanding.

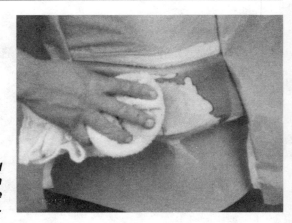

Mask the entire area and clean it again with wax-and-silicone remover.

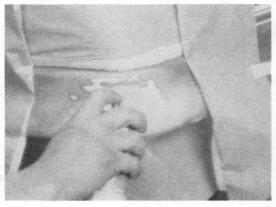

Spray the area with automotive primer. *Wet sand it with 400- or 600-grit sandpaper. If necessary, spray and sand again to get a perfect surface.*

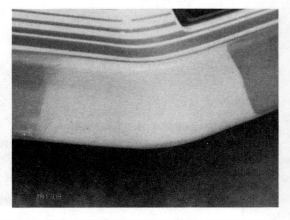

The finished job, ready for final paint. *The crack in the ABS plastic is gone, the surface is ultra-smooth, and there's no evidence that there was any damage—other than the primer. See Section 10 for instructions on painting.*

Section 9:

How to Repair Minor Rust Damage

There are very few places in the United States where vehicles won't rust to some degree or other. In the snowy northern states, destructive rust perforation is often accelerated by road salt. Salt air in coastal areas can cause rust damage, although this type rarely causes structural problems. And anywhere it rains, rust can happen.

In this section we show you how to repair minor rust damage with fiberglass cloth and resin. For this book, we define "minor rust damage" as spots no larger than 2 to 3 inches in diameter. (Bigger holes should be repaired by a professional.) Fix rust damage when you first spot it, and save yourself big money and headaches!

Fiberglass is excellent for rust repairs. It's inexpensive, easy to handle, and virtually ensures that rust won't reoccur in the repaired area.

The illustration below gives you an overview of the step-by-step rust repair process. It is particularly important to see how the edges of the metal are bent inward to keep them from showing through the final repair.

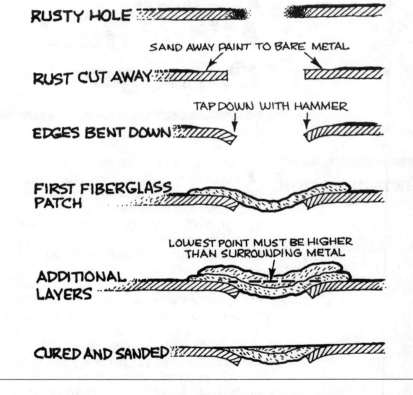

RUSTY HOLE

RUST CUT AWAY
SAND AWAY PAINT TO BARE METAL

EDGES BENT DOWN
TAP DOWN WITH HAMMER

FIRST FIBERGLASS PATCH

ADDITIONAL LAYERS
LOWEST POINT MUST BE HIGHER THAN SURROUNDING METAL

CURED AND SANDED

Overview of the rust repair process. This is a cross-section view, showing how the patch is built up and then sanded down.

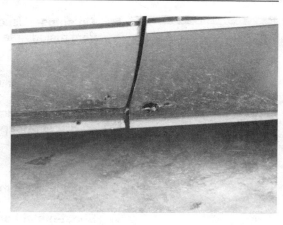

BEFORE:
Typical body panel rust.
Visible rust is only the tip of the iceberg. There's probably a half inch more under the paint around each hole.

AFTER:
A strong, permanent repair, ready for final color painting. *The rusted metal has been cut away and replaced with a strong, permanent fiberglass cloth patch. Your savings? Several hundred dollars!*

This pickup truck is from sunny southern California! Yet even in this climate, the body became perforated with rust.

WARNING: Fiberglass can be very harmful to your health. You must observe the precautions given on page 107 to protect yourself.

TOOLS AND SUPPLIES

■ **Tin snips**—Used to remove sheet metal from rusted area.

■ **Chalk, crayon, or felt marker**—To mark the sheet metal to be removed.

■ **Electric drill motor, sanding disc, and 40-grit sandpaper**—Used to prepare the surface.

■ **Rust dissolver**—To remove excess rust from the sheet metal surface.

■ **Sheet-metal hammer**—Used to knock down edges of holes in the sheet metal.

■ **Masking paper and masking tape**—To protect the area surrounding the repair.

■ **Fiberglass patch repair kit (fiberglass cloth, resin, hardener)**—Used to patch rust holes.

■ **Wax-and-silicone remover**—For cleaning the metal surface.

■ **Flexible sanding block, 40-, 80-, 200-, and 400-grit sandpaper**—Used to sand and finish the repair area.

■ **Body filler**—Used to fill imperfections in the fiberglass repair.

■ **Automotive primer**—Used to cover the repair and prepare it for final paint.

■ **Glazing and spot putty**—Used to fill pinholes prior to final priming and painting.

HOW TO PREPARE THE SHEET METAL

Rust repair is a two-part job. First, you must remove *all* the metal that's been attacked by rust. Rust is like cancer, and if you don't remove all of it from the damaged area, it will rust through again. Second, you must reconstruct the damaged area with fiberglass because you will create an even larger hole when you cut away all the damaged metal. Working with fiberglass is only a little more involved than working with plastic body filler. The fiberglass repair should last the lifetime of the vehicle and stop any further rust damage in the repaired area.

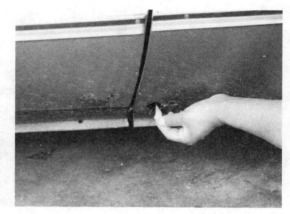

Pull out all the leaves and debris from the hole and behind the panel. Be careful not to cut your fingers on the sharp edges.

Cut away the obvious rusted sheet metal with tin snips. This will help you get a better idea of what's going on and see how extensive the damage is.

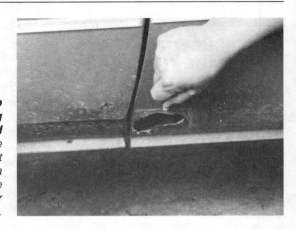

Draw a box or circle to guide you in cutting away the rust around the hole. You may have to enlarge it after you get the paint off, but this is a good start. Here, we marked a rectangular area to guide our cutting.

Cut along the outline with the snips, and completely remove the rusty section.

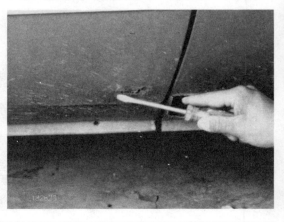

Where you find rust, there's usually more close by. In this case, in the lower section of the door. A little exploratory scraping with a screwdriver showed it was more extensive than we originally thought.

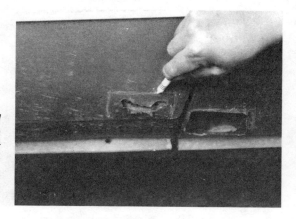

Again, mark the rusted area to be cut away. *This helps as a guide for your tin snips and keeps you within the rust, so you don't remove any more material than necessary.*

Remove the rusted area with tin snips. *This section has a door reinforcement rib behind it, making cutting a little slower—but still necessary and worthwhile.*

Remove the paint from the surrounding area. *Use 40-grit sandpaper on your drill-motor disc sander.*

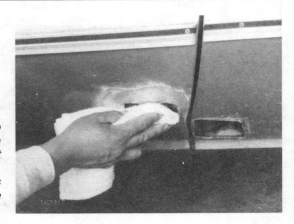

Apply rust dissolver to any metal inside, such as the reinforcement behind this door panel. Don't wipe it off. This helps stop any future rust formation.

All of this debris came out of the hole on the right! The rust was caused by leaves and moisture. What looks like dirt is actually a combination of decomposed leaves and rust—deadly to sheet metal!

Tap down the edges of each hole. *Make sure the metal is lower than the final surface. (See the illustration on page 122.) This also allows the fiberglass cloth to get a better grip, and makes a smoother transition from fiberglass to sheet metal.*

Cover the area below the repair with masking paper. *Fiberglass work is a messy process, and this confines it to the area being repaired.*

PREPARE FIBERGLASS PATCHES

It's important to prepare the patches for your repair ahead of time. Once the resin and hardener have been mixed, they start curing almost immediately. There's no time then to cut and fit patches to the hole.

Cut out a piece of fiberglass cloth that is just slightly larger than the hole. *A deep hole, such as this one, will require four to six layers of fiberglass for the repair.*

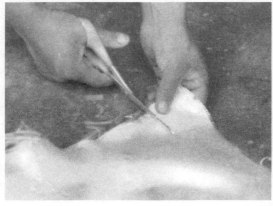

Cut all your patches before mixing the resin. *Each piece of cloth should be larger than the previous one. Put the smallest one against the metal, and work your way out with increasingly larger pieces.*

HOW TO MIX RESIN

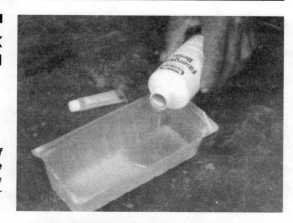

Pour a small amount of resin into a disposable mixing container. *Use enough to saturate your fiberglass cloth patches.*

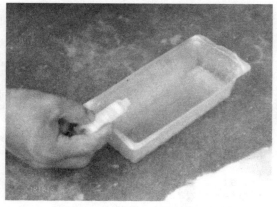

Add a few drops of hardener in accordance with the directions in the kit. *This hardener causes a chemical reaction that immediately starts hardening the resin. Follow the instructions carefully. The more hardener you use, the faster the resin hardens.*

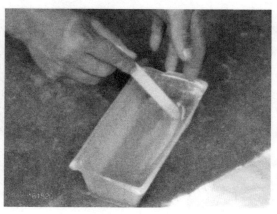

Mix the hardener thoroughly with a wooden stick. *Thorough mixing helps to eliminate pinholes in the finished job. You can tell it's done when it reaches a dark green color, and has a syrup-like consistency. Continue your work quickly because the hardening process has begun.*

HOW TO APPLY THE PATCHES

Dip the first fiberglass cloth patch into the resin. *Turn it over several times to make sure it's thoroughly saturated with resin. Note that you should use rubber gloves to keep the resin off your skin.*

Put the patch over the hole. *It's slippery and will slide around, so you'll have to use your fingers to help hold it in place.*

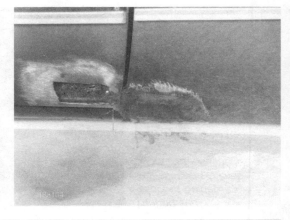

This is the way the repair should look with the first layer of the patch in place. *It's okay for the fiberglass to sink in the center. It will be filled later.*

Apply additional layers of cloth to the repair, each one larger than the last. These layers of cloth add strength to the repair and build up the area.

The second hole receives its patch—a total of only four layers of cloth were needed. Because this patch is supported by the door reinforcement, it doesn't sink in like the first repair.

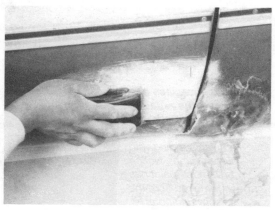

After the fiberglass has completely cured, begin sanding the excess with 40-grit sandpaper. See page 116 for curing time estimates. Use a sanding block.

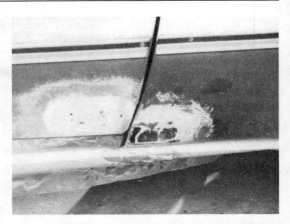

The patch on the right has two large depressions where the fiberglass has sunk inward. This is a common situation in rust repair. Note how the edges of the patches have already been feathered somewhat into the adjacent sheet metal.

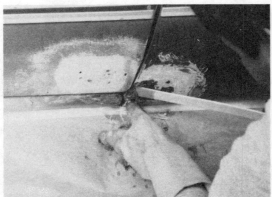

Fill large depressions with a new batch of resin and fiberglass cloth. Here, cut smaller patches to fit inside the depression, or use a small "wad" of cloth. Tiny depressions can be filled with resin alone. It took several applications for this particular repair.

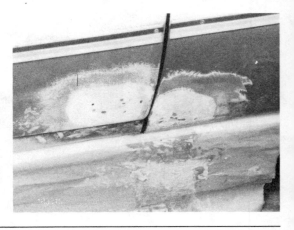

When the fiberglass has cured, the repair is sanded smooth with 80-grit paper, followed by a finish sanding with 200-grit paper. Notice how much paint has been removed from the surrounding area.

PRO TIP: Fiberglass Tips and Shortcuts that Don't Work

In cases where there is no backing (like our example hole in the fender), some people suggest a few "tricks" to keep the fiberglass from falling into the hole and creating a depression. One "secret" is to glue a piece of cardboard behind the hole, so the fiberglass has something to adhere to. Another popular tip is to fill the hole with plain steel wool before patching.

But both methods can cause a major problem. Both the cardboard and steel wool absorb moisture and can promote new rust within weeks.

The best way to patch a hole that has no support is to continue "packing in" layers of fiberglass to build up the hole until the repair is level with the surface of the surrounding sheet metal. We know of no other method that guarantees "no more rust."

HOW TO FINISH THE RUST REPAIR

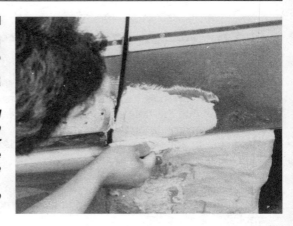

Mix body filler and hardener, and apply it to the fiberglass repair area. *Very little should be necessary if you've done a good job on your patch. See Section 4 for how to mix and apply filler.*

Once the filler has dried, sand the area with an 80-grit sandpaper. *If the surface is still rough or has small depressions, mix up another batch of filler and apply it. Be sure to use a flexible sanding block.*

Finish the surface with a 200-grit sandpaper, and feather the edges of the body filler. *Check the surface with your hand for an absolutely smooth job, with no waves.*

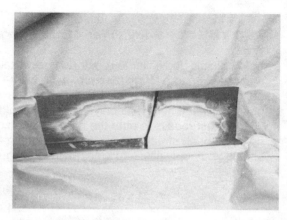

Mask off the repair area completely. *The Pro Tip on page 143 gives details on masking.*

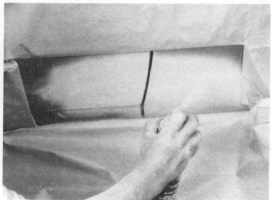

Use a spray can of automotive primer to seal the repair area. *Check for pinholes, sanding scratches, and "cat claw" marks. If necessary, use glazing and spot putty to perfect the surface, as described on page 92. Then spray on another coat of primer.*

The finished job! *You'd never know that there was rust here before—and it will never come back! Instructions for finish painting are given in the next section.*

PRO TIP: Why Body Filler Alone Won't Work on Rust

Using plastic body filler to repair rust holes seems like a quick and easy solution to a tough problem. It will work—for a while—until the next rain, when the sponge-like filler absorbs water, swells, and pops out of the hole! The only time you should use plastic body filler on rust repairs is after the rust has been removed, and the hole has been structurally repaired with fiberglass. Only then should you apply filler—to smooth small irregularities in the fiberglass.

Here's what happens when you take a short-cut. This rusted area was covered with filler which peeled away and may soon fall out. The job has to be completely redone.

How to Paint Small Areas With a Spray Can

This section shows you two examples of typical paint jobs with a spray can. The first example, beginning on the next page, assumes that your dent repair is complete and ready for final primer and paint. The second example, beginning on page 163, shows the complete procedure for repairing a large scratch, using primer to fill the surface. This procedure also shows you how to use a "paint block" for smaller areas.

All the painting techniques shown in this section use automotive primer and paint in common aerosol spray cans. Obviously the pros use expensive spray guns and compressors. But by carefully following the techniques shown here, you too can get professional results at a fraction of the cost.

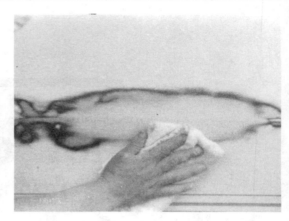

BEFORE:
One dent, or a dozen,
the solution is the same.
This door dent has been pulled and filled. The filler has been sanded to shape and feathered. It's now ready for a finishing paint job.

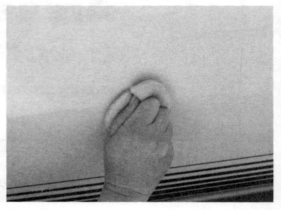

AFTER:
A perfect invisible paint job *using aerosol cans of automotive primer and paint. The trick to a perfect finish is careful preparation before painting and careful color-sanding and rubbing.*

The most common mistakes made by a new do-it-yourselfer are: (1) poor surface preparation, (2) failure to use primer, and (3) spraying color paint in a single thick layer rather than a number of thin coats. If you have a clear-coat finish, your last layer or two should be clear spray paint. The final gloss of your paint job comes a week later—with wet-sanding and polishing compound.

TOOLS AND SUPPLIES

■ **Wax-and-silicone remover**—Used to clean the surface before painting.

■ **Flexible sanding block and 1000-grit wet/dry sandpaper**—Used for final sanding of the primer before painting and for wet-sanding of the final color or clear-coat paint.

■ **Masking tape and masking paper**—Protects against overspray.

■ **Automotive primer paint**—Seals and prepares the area for finish paint.

■ **Glazing and spot putty**—For filling small pinholes in the primer.

■ **Plastic applicator**—Used to apply glazing and spot putty.

■ **Tack cloth**—To remove dust.

■ **Automotive color paint**—Make sure it is the exact color of your vehicle. See page 4 for how to match.

■ **Clear-coat paint**—Only if your vehicle has a clear-coat finish.

■ **Polishing compound**—Used to shine the cured paint after wet-sanding.

■ **Carnauba wax**—Used to protect the finished repair.

■ **100% cotton T-shirt or terry cloth rags**—For compound and wax.

FINISH SANDING

Wet-sand the area to be painted. *Use 1000-grit wet sandpaper on your block to make sure the surface is absolutely smooth. Check with your hand.*

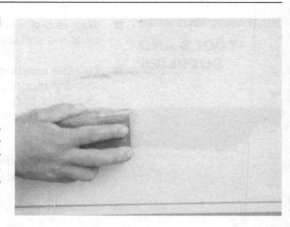

Reclean the entire area with wax-and-silicone remover. *This will ensure that no grinding dust or dirt will get into your finished paint job.*

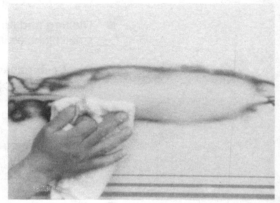

PRO TIP: How to Mask Like a Pro

Most of the repairs shown in this book require you to paint only a portion of a body panel. To get a soft edge with both primer and color paint, use the technique shown here.

Always use real masking tape—not duct tape, sealing tape, or transparent tape. We also recommend you use real masking paper, which will not absorb paint like newspaper does. In a pinch, butcher paper works fine, but costs more.

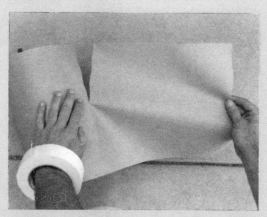

Tear off four pieces of masking paper, larger than the dent repair area.

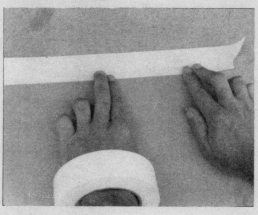

Apply masking tape along one edge of the paper. This is easy to do on a clean floor or pavement. Make sure the tape adheres well to the paper.

Apply the paper just above the dent repair area. Place it just above all bare metal and sanding. Note how the paper actually covers the repair area (in white) at this time.

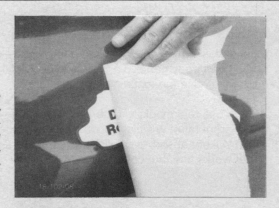

Here's the trick: pull the paper up...

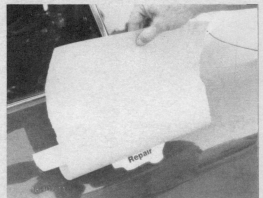

And tape it down, leaving a soft rolled edge next to the dent repair area. This method of reverse taping prevents a hard line from forming in either the primer or the color paint. It makes sanding and blending much easier and faster.

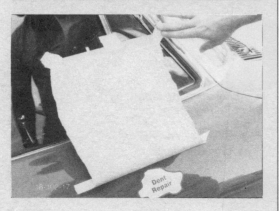

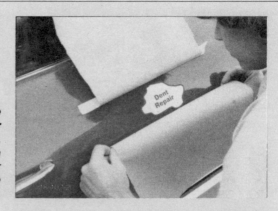

Apply a second piece of masking paper below the repair area. Note how you can sight over the paper to get it into the proper position.

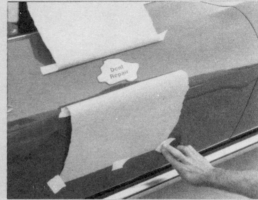

Tape the second piece to hold it down with the soft edge next to the repair.

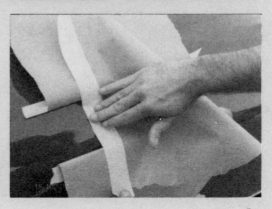

Tape the third piece of masking paper to the left side of the repair.

Fold the third piece back and tape it down.

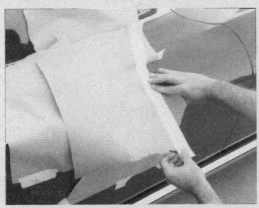

And finally, tape the fourth piece to the right side of the repair.

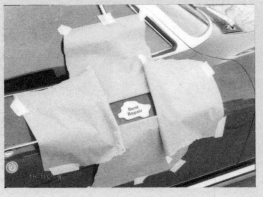

Fold it back, tape it down, and the job is done. Note how the surrounding area is totally protected from overspray, yet the rolled edges around the repair area will produce a softer edge in the paint.

AEROSOL SPRAY PAINTING TECHNIQUE

Priming and painting with aerosol paint cans is where many jobs go wrong. In spite of all your hard and careful work, incorrect technique with either primer or color paint can produce a poor finish and spoil an otherwise great repair job. Understanding the right spraying and finishing techniques is essential for producing a smooth, glossy finish.

We recommend that you practice your spraying on a scrap piece of cardboard. Learn to apply a nice, even thin coat before you proceed to your vehicle.

Always shake the can thoroughly before spraying. *Most manufacturers recommend at least 1 minute. We recommend 2 minutes. Shake in a rapid clockwise and counter-clockwise motion—not up and down. This is known as the "pharmacist" shake.*

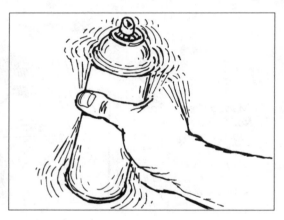

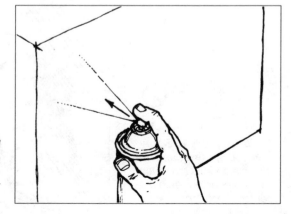

Hold the can parallel and square to the surface you'll be spraying. Keep your wrist locked.

Spray with the nozzle about 8 inches from the surface and with your arm and wrist locked. Make believe there's a cast on your wrist, and it can't be moved at all! Use body English (moving your entire body) to move back and forth.

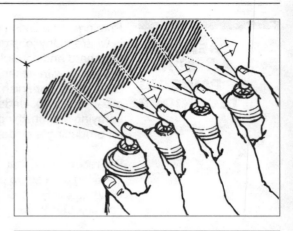

Wrong Way to Spray No. 1. The wrist is bent and the can is moved from right to left by swinging the hand. This puts lots of paint in the middle, and very little on the edges.

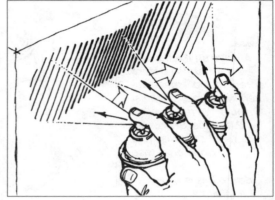

Wrong Way to Spray No. 2. Spraying up and down also puts too much paint or primer in the center of your spray area.

The results of a tipped can. *Spraying with the can tipped down slightly will put more paint on the top portion of the repair and not enough at the bottom. The opposite problem occurs if the can is tipped up.*

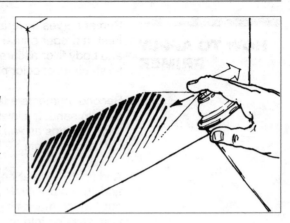

Start spraying while the nozzle is pointed at the masking paper. *Don't stop until you've reached the paper on the other side. There should be as much paint on the paper as on the surface you're painting.*

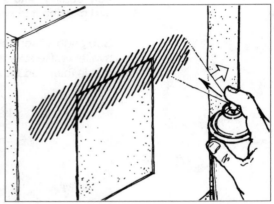

Release the nozzle at the end of each stroke. *Then, press and hold the nozzle as you start back in the other direction. You'll quickly find the rhythm. If you simply hold the nozzle down and move the can back and forth, paint will build up at the end of each stroke.*

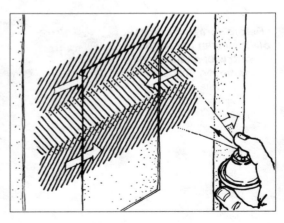

HOW TO APPLY PRIMER

Primer serves several important functions. First, a proper primer base over sheet metal and body filler assures a strong bond for the finish coats of color paint.

Second, primer is a fast-drying filler that is easy to sand. It allows you to fill small imperfections as you apply and sand successive coats.

And finally, primer helps your final paint dry and cure properly. Primer performs as a "hold out," which means it prevents your final paint from soaking into the body filler, softening it and causing it to sink.

See page 17 for details on the types of primer available. Be sure to buy good quality primer that is intended for automotive use.

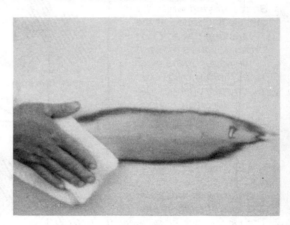

Before spraying primer, always clean the surface with wax-and-silicone remover. Then wipe it with a tack cloth.

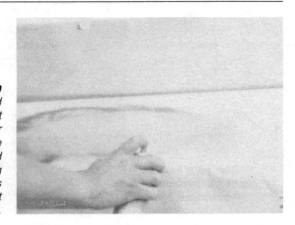

Spray on the first thin coat of primer. *It should be very thin, and just barely "mist" the repair area. You should be able to still see filler and original paint showing through this coat. Let this coat of primer dry for at least 10 minutes.*

Apply several more thin coats of primer. *After the second coat, filler should still show through. The third coat should barely cover the area, and the fourth coat should completely cover it. Allow at least 10 minutes for each coat to dry.*

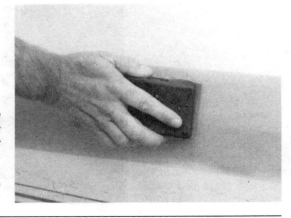

Remove the masking paper and lightly block sand the primer *with wet 400- or 600-grit sandpaper. Allow it to dry, then clean the surface to remove any residue.*

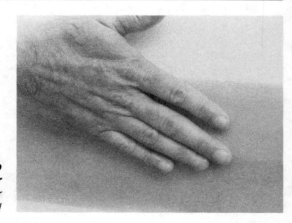

Use your hand to check the surface for smoothness. *Never trust your eyes!*

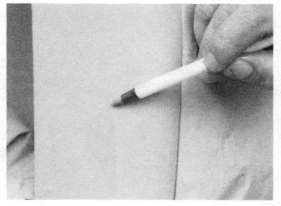

Why use your hand? Here's a good example in another repair job. *We could feel small pits and low spots here, but we couldn't SEE them. If you can feel a blemish with your hand, it will show up in your final paint job. How to fix?*

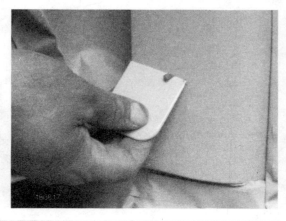

Glazing and spot putty is the solution for any small pits and low spots. *Glazing putty is like thick primer paint, and is essential at this stage for a quality final finish.*

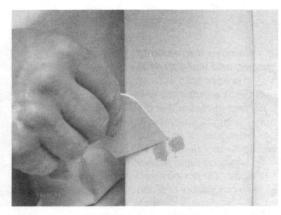

Apply the putty to the surface in a single, very thin layer. Push down hard to force the putty into the surface. The putty will be about as thick as a piece of paper when applied correctly. Work quickly. The putty dries fast and is hard to work after it's exposed to air for a few minutes.

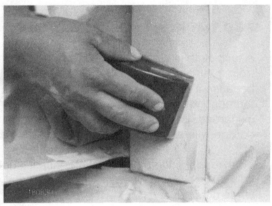

Lightly wet-sand the spot putty with 400- or 600-grit sandpaper. Decrease the amount of pressure near the edges to feather them. Wet the sandpaper a couple of times a minute. Keep the surface wet by squeezing a sponge above the repair area.

Back to our original door repair, remask the area and apply primer over the spot putty. Use several thin coats of primer, allowing at least 10 minutes of drying time for each one.

Remove the masking paper, and wet-sand the primer with 400- or 600-grit sandpaper to a perfect surface. Wet the sandpaper every 30 seconds or so. If you discover any defects, use spot putty and primer again. Do not proceed with color paint until the surface is perfect.

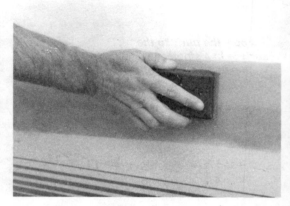

PRO TIP: Keeping a Tack Cloth Alive

A tack cloth is essential for removing unseen grit, lint, and dust from a surface about to be painted. A tack cloth does its job well because it's made of a special close-weave, chemically treated material. When it becomes dirty with use, it must eventually be discarded. However, just sitting unprotected on a shelf in the garage will reduce its lifespan to just a few days.

To extend the life of a tack cloth once it's been removed from its original packaging, always keep it in a tightly sealed plastic bag when not in use.

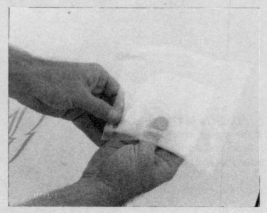

To extend the life of a tack cloth, keep it in a sealed plastic bag. This keeps it from attracting dust or lint from the air.

HOW TO APPLY COLOR AND CLEAR-COAT PAINT

Paint must be built up in layers, or coats. You'll start with a very light first coat and progress to slightly heavier coats, until the final color coverage is complete. A final layer of clear-coat is necessary if it is on the finish you're matching. See page 147 for spraying techniques.

A common mistake is applying a thick, wet, glossy coat which sags and runs. When done correctly, the final gloss is achieved by wet sanding and polishing the paint after it has thoroughly cured.

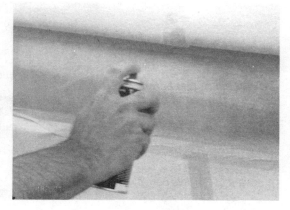

Remask the area, wipe it with a tack cloth, and spray on an extremely light coat of color paint. *You should still be able to see more primer than finish paint at this point. Wait 10 minutes.*

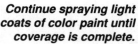

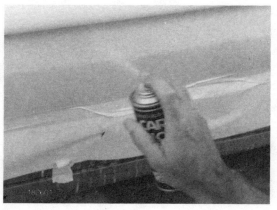

Continue spraying light coats of color paint until coverage is complete. *Allow each coat to dry at least 30-60 minutes. If you are not going to use clear-coat, make sure your color base has enough coats for subsequent wet sanding. (We applied five light coats of color here.)*

If applying clear-coat:
Allow your final color coat to dry for about 30 minutes, then spray a very light coat of clear. When that coat is tacky or dry, spray a slightly wetter finishing coat. Let the final finish cure for at least one week before doing a final polish (see page 160).

Clean the nozzle before storing the can of paint.
Turn the can upside-down and spray for 3 to 5 seconds, just until paint quits coming out of the nozzle. Next time you want to use this can, it will be ready to go!

PRO TIP: How to Use an Inexpensive Airbrush for Paint Touch-Up

Every once in a while someone improves on a basic concept and makes life simpler. The B&M Paint Perfect system is just such a concept. It is easy to work with, not very expensive, and can produce fine results. The Paint Perfect gets its air from one of your vehicle's tires. The sprayer uses only about 4 psi to do a small repair area. You can overinflate your tire just before starting the job, or use your spare tire. If you can't find the B&M Paint Perfect in your area, airbrushes are also available at hobby shops.

The B&M Paint Perfect includes the airbrush, 6 feet of air hose, an adapter, and three bottles of chemicals—Activator, Paint Prep, and Spray Finish. Connect the sprayer adapter to your vehicle's tire.

Fill the glass bottle on the spray gun about half full with the matching paint.

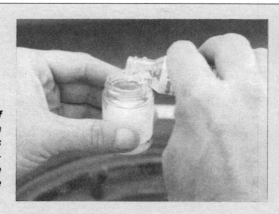

Add eight drops of Paint Activator, which comes with the kit. This is a catalyst, or hardener. Attach the hose to the gun, and you're ready to begin.

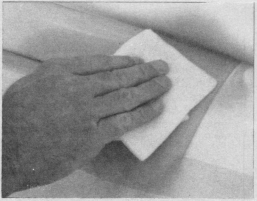

Apply Paint Prep to the repair area, and wipe it with a soft cloth. This is similar to wax-and-silicone remover; it prepares the surface for painting.

Experiment with the spray gun on a piece of cardboard to get a feel for how it covers. Adjust the airflow by turning the needle on the tire adapter clockwise. Adjust the paint flow by turning the paint nozzle tip counterclockwise for less paint, or clockwise for more paint.

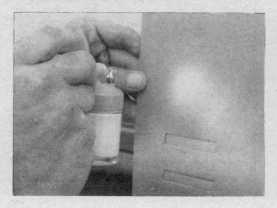

Hold the gun 3 to 4 inches from the surface you're painting. *This is closer than you'd hold a spray can and allows you to do smaller areas without overspray. Since the airbrush sprays such a small amount of paint, five or six coats equals four coats from a spray can.*

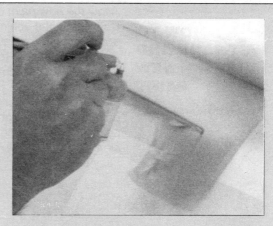

The finished job! *The airbrush does a nice job of blending and laying down a smoother surface than aerosol paint. You still may need to wet-sand and compound for final gloss, however.*

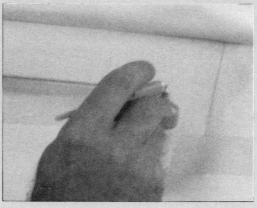

After the paint has dried, use the Spray Finish that's supplied with the airbrush to wipe off any excess paint. This may not be necessary if you've followed the other steps carefully.

HOW TO WET-SAND AND POLISH NEW PAINT

Allow the new paint to dry for at least a week. Don't wash the vehicle, and don't set anything on the painted area. The surface may be hard to the touch, but the layers under the surface could still be slightly soft.

Only after a week or more of curing will the paint be hard enough for wet-sanding and polishing. Be very careful when wet-sanding clear-coat. It is softer than color paint and easy to damage.

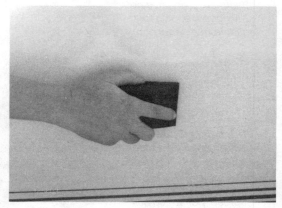

Wet-sand the paint lightly with 1000-grit paper. Use lots of water. Sand the area as little as possible. When the surface is glassy smooth, you're done. Dry the area.

Use polishing compound thinned with water to further shine the surface. Rub lightly, and check your progress often. Do not rub through the clear-coat. When finished, clean the area thoroughly to remove all traces of compound.

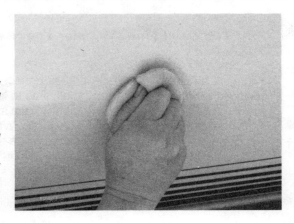

Finish polishing the new paint with a glaze, and apply a coat of wax. Glaze contains an ultrafine abrasive and chemicals to fill minute scratches. Your finish wax may also contain a cleaner, but we prefer a 100% wax product.

Congratulations! You've done a professional-level paint job and saved yourself a pile of money. Plus, you've gained a useful skill that can return benefits through your entire life.

(If you would like to know more about glazing and waxing your entire vehicle, see the companion book in this Do-It-Right Professional Tips and Techniques Series: *Detailing Cars and Trucks.*)

PRO TIP: Can't Find the Color You Need In a Spray Can?

You have a relatively small dent repair project, but can't find the correct color in an aerosol can? Well, time to let your fingers do the walking. Call a professional automotive paint supply store—one that supplies paint to your local bodyshops. With your paint code number (see page 5), they can custom-mix a quart for you. This is going to be more expensive and less convenient than buying an aerosol can, but at least it will match. How to apply it? Try an airbrush (see page 157) or try this solution...

Use a pressurized bottle for spraying paint on small repairs. These bottles are widely available for less than $5 and do a pretty good job of applying the paint evenly. You'll still have to wet-sand and polish, as shown on the preceding page.

SPECIAL TECHNIQUES FOR REPAIRING AND PAINTING A SMALL AREA

These next few pages show you another typical repair and painting project. This large scratch was deep enough to go through the primer to the sheet metal. The sheet metal was *not* dented, however. Rather than just brush on touch-up paint, we decided to sand the area smooth, fill it with a heavy primer, and spray-paint the color. This project also shows you how to use a paint block instead of masking paper.

This large scratch on a gas-filler door carries over onto the body panel. *Both paint and primer were damaged. This scratch must first be filled and leveled with primer before it can be painted.*

Feather the scratch with 400-grit sandpaper. *Remove just enough material to blend the paint with the primer and the primer with the bare sheet metal.*

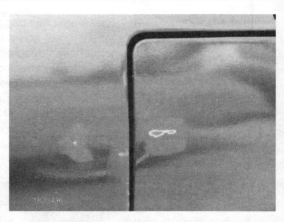

Make sure the scratch is absolutely smooth. Here you can see the feathered paint, primer, and metal. (We discovered some old chips along the gas-filler door opening, and feathered them as well.)

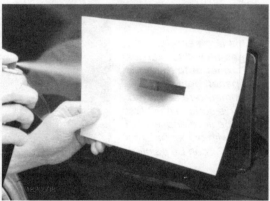

Build up the repair with primer. Shoot through a paint block. This will confine the primer to the repair area and permit it to feather out naturally on the edges. Red oxide primer was used for this dark brown metallic finish.

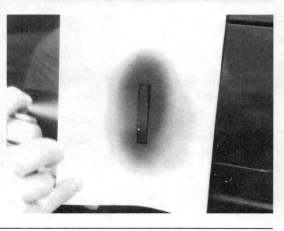

Turn the paint block to the vertical to prime the edge of the door. Allow the primer to dry for at least 10 minutes, and then spray on a second coat.

How to Paint Small Areas with a Spray Can

PRO TIP: Save Time and Effort With a Paint Block

A quick and simple way to control paint spray during touchup is to use a paint block. This is simply a stiff piece of cardboard with an appropriate hole cut in it. To use the block, hold it about 1/2 inch from the surface you're painting, and spray through the hole.

Not only does a paint block eliminate the need for masking, but it also does a great job of controlling the spray pattern. The troublesome spatter of large drops of paint occurs mostly at the outer edges of the spray fan. When a paint block is used, these drops hit it, and only the fine spray at the center reaches the surface.

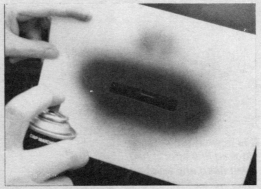

A paint block works great for directing paint onto this thin spot on a fender edge. Once cured, this type of repair requires only a light polish to feather it into the surrounding paint.

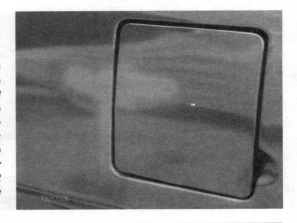

This is what the scratch should look like with it's completely filled. Several coats may be required to get it to this point. Notice how the paint block has confined the primer to the repair area. Allow the repair to dry for at least 1 hour before block sanding it.

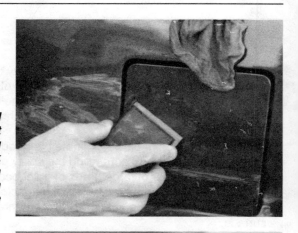

Wet-sand the filled repair with 400-grit paper on a sanding block. *Check your work often, and stop as soon as the area is smooth and level with the surrounding paint.*

This is what the scratch looked like after it had been filled and leveled. *There were still a few tiny imperfections in the repair.*

Prime the repair again. *Remember—build up several thin coats rather than one thick one.*

How to Paint Small Areas with a Spray Can

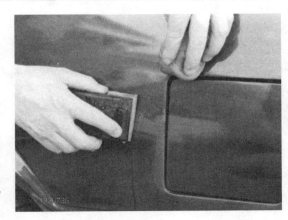

Block sand the area again. This time, the primer filled the remaining imperfections and the area was ready for final paint.

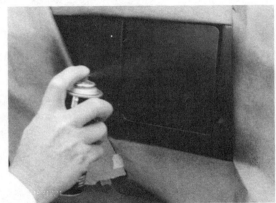

Mask and paint the repair. Follow the procedures already given in this section.

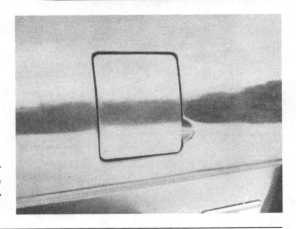

The final result! Another perfect job using inexpensive aerosol spray primer and paint.

INDEX

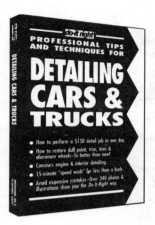
CONTENTS: 1 The Detailing Process: • Overview of a total detail job **2 Understanding Detailing Products:** • Choosing a chamois • Understanding paint cleaner ("deoxidizer"), polish ("glaze"), and carnauba wax • Understanding one-step cleaner-wax • Understanding wheel cleaners, metal polish, and other specialized products • Should you buy an electric orbital buffer? • Assembling a proper wash kit and detailing kit **3 Professional Hand Wash:** • Preparation • Proper washing and drying technique • Glass cleaning secrets • Interior and exterior finishing **4 Conserve Water: the Two-Bucket Wash** • Preparation • Washing technique **5 Paint Detailing:** • How to restore badly weathered paint • How to clean, polish, glaze, and wax conventional paint, clear-coat paint, and show-quality lacquer paint (3 case studies) **6 Trim Detailing:** • How to properly polish chrome and other metal trim • Special techniques and products for polishing plastic and metallized plastic trim • How to clean and preserve rubber and vinyl trim • How to restore trim backgrounds and metallized plastic **7 Convertible Top Detailing:** • How to shampoo and preserve convertible tops • How to clean plastic windows **8 Professional Tire and Wheel Detailing:** • Tire detailing • How to select and use spray-on wheel cleaners • How to detail chrome wheels, painted steel wheels, wire wheels and covers • How to detail wheel wells • How to touch up wheel cover accents **9 Professional Interior Detailing:** • Vinyl seats and trim • Fabric Seats and trim • Leather seats and trim • Carpet cleaning • Door detailing • Dashboard detailing • Seat belt cleaning • Trunk detailing **10 Professional Underhood Detailing:** • Driveway engine washing • Engine painting • Polishing and protecting • Professional extra touches **11 Truck Chassis Detailing:** • Blazer project • Ford truck project **12 The 15-Minute Quick Wash:** • Fast wash, dry, and finish **13 Time Saving One-Step Cleaner-Wax Job:** • Applying and deoxidizing • Buffing and shining • Finishing touches.

TUNE-UP CONTENTS: 1 Tune-Up Overview:
• The correct steps and sequence for a tune-up
• Tuning a modern electronic engine **2 Tune-Up Parts, Supplies and Tools:** • Examination of what you need **3 Valve Adjustment:** • How mechanical and hydraulic valve lifters work • How to fix noisy lifters **4 Compression Test:** • How to perform dry and wet compression tests • How to interpret test results **5 Spark Plugs:** • Reading engine condition • How to know if you need hotter or colder spark plugs • How to prepare and install new plugs **6 Distributor and Wires:** • How to test spark plug wires • How to assemble "universal" wire kits • How to install new ignition wires • How to inspect, test, and service the distributor • How to use a tach/dwell meter • How to check and adjust ignition timing **7 Carburetor/ Fuel Injection:** • How to clean a carburetor • How to clean and inspect a fuel-injection system • How to replace the fuel filter(s) • How to inspect and test a PCV system • How to replace the air filter • How to adjust idle speed • Oldies only— fast-idle and mixture adjustment.

ELECTRICAL SERVICE CONTENTS:
8 Electrical Parts, Supplies and Tools: • A look at what you need **9 Battery:** • How a battery works and what can go wrong • How to inspect and service the battery • How to test condition with a hydrometer • How to select and replace • How to charge • How to measure and replace battery cables **10 Lamps and Wiring:** • How to replace sealed-beam and quartz-halogen headlamps • How to upgrade tungsten headlamps to quartz-halogen • How to aim headlamps • How to replace exterior and interior lamp bulbs • How to troubleshoot bulb burnout problems • How to replace damaged wires and sockets **11 Fuses and Circuit Breakers:** • How to inspect and replace fuses and fusible links • How to install an in-line fuse holder **12 Charging System:** • How to troubleshoot problems in the alternator and charging system • How to replace the alternator **13 Starting System:** • How to troubleshoot starter problems • How to replace the starter.

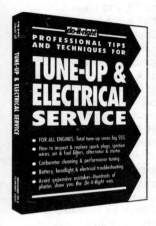

This is a complete guide to two types of important DIY jobs.
Part A, Tune-Up, gives you a 5-step procedure for inspecting and tuning virtually any gasoline engine. Part B, Electrical Service, shows you how to perform a number of easy, money-saving electrical jobs.

192 pages, 219 illustrations
ISBN 1-879110-15-6

This book gives you instructions for a complete professional lubrication service. *It also includes instruction for a number of important chassis maintenance and repair jobs. There is a chapter on special considerations for 4-wheel-drive vehicles.*

192 pages, 236 illustrations
ISBN 1-879110-16-4

LUBRICATION CONTENTS: 1 Save Money with Frequent Maintenance: • Why more frequent maintenance costs less • How to keep you vehicle under warranty with DIY work **2 Parts, Supplies, and Tools:** • The rundown on what you need **3 Engine Oil and Filter Change:** • How to select the best oil and additives • Is synthetic oil right for your engine? • How to read oil condition • How to change oil and filter correctly **4 Steering and Suspension:** • How to install permanent grease fittings • How to lube steering and suspension • How to inspect for bushing wear • How to replace constant-velocity (CV) joint boots • How to check springs and torsion bars **5 Transmission and Drivetrain:** • How to change manual transmission oil • How to interpret fluid condition • How to change automatic transmission fluid and screen "leak-free" • How to inspect and change differential oil • How to lube driveshaft slip joints • How to service front wheel bearings **6 Four-Wheel Drive:** • How to change differential oil • How to change transfer case oil • How to lube slip joints and front-axle CV-joints

CHASSIS MAINTENANCE CONTENTS: 7 Drive Belts: • How to inspect and adjust • How to select the correct type • How to replace • How to put together a "free" emergency belt kit **8 Cooling System:** • Complete cooling system "tune-up" • How to test coolant freeze-protection capability • How to install a permanent coolant flushing fitting • How to reverse-flush the cooling system • How to inspect and replace radiator and heater hoses • How to replace the thermostat **9 Brake System:** • How to check and replenish brake fluid • How to inspect disk brake pads and rotor • How to fix squealing disk brakes • How to inspect and replace brake fluid • How to bleed a brake system • How to flush and replace the fluid **10 Shock Absorbers:** • How to test shock and strut condition • How to select and replace • Understanding mountings **11 Exhaust System:** • How to inspect the complete exhaust system **12 Body:** • How to lubricate body hinges and latches • How to select and replace wipers.

ORDER FORM & INFORMATION REQUEST

We recommend you purchase Do-It-Right books from your local retailer, where you purchased this book. But if you would like to order from us or add your name to our mailing list for future product announcements, please use this form.

Name: _____

Address: _____

_____

City: _____ State: _____ Zip: _____

Daytime phone: _____
(in case we have to call about this order)

Mail to:
Do-It-Right Publishing
Post Office Box 839
Newhall, CA 91322-0839

Credit card orders, call toll-free:
1-800-223-3556
9-5 Pacific Time, Monday-Friday
(In California: **1-800-445-4944**)

Title	Price Each	Quantity	Total
Tune-Up & Electrical Service	$8.95		
Lube, Oil & Chassis Service	$8.95		
Detailing Cars & Trucks	$8.95		
Touch-Up & Dent Repair	$8.95		
Total book order			
California residents: 6.5% tax (58¢ per book)			
Shipping & handling per order			$1.95
TOTAL AMOUNT			

Paid by: ❏ Check ❏ Master Charge ❏ Visa ❏ American Express

Make checks payable to **Do-It-Right**.

Account No:_____ Expiration date: _____

Your Signature: _____

Orders are shipped immediately. Please allow several weeks for delivery.

❏ Please add me to your mailing list for new book and video announcements.

❏ Please send me a brochure on your model-specific factory-approved DIY manuals and shop manuals for: ❏ Nissan vehicles ❏ Hyundai vehicles.

Over for your comments.

Your comments on this *Touch-Up & Dent Repair* manual would be appreciated.

_____

_____

_____

_____

I rate this book
❏ Excellent ❏ Very Good ❏ OK ❏ Poor

Other titles I would like to see from Do-It-Right:

_____ ❏ Book ❏ Video

_____ ❏ Book ❏ Video

FOLD HERE AND STAPLE OR TAPE SHUT

_____

_____

_____

```
PLACE
STAMP
HERE
```

Do-It-Right Publishing
Post Office Box 839
Newhall, CA 91322-0839

Do-It-Right Books are Different. Here is Why.

"After training factory technicians for 18 years, we wanted to bring the same type of concise job-specific training to DIYer's. This Professional Tips and Techniques Series is the result. We hope you enjoy it."

Photos and Illustrations Tell the Story. We believe that automotive instruction should be as *visual* as possible, because do-it-yourself work is a visual, hands-on process. We begin every book with a storyboard plan and a camera full of film. Our goal is to *show* you rather than to *tell* you how to do each job.

We Focus on Real-World Money-Saving Jobs. In our judgment, each job must (1) be easy for a DIYer to do with ordinary tools and skills, (2) have low risk of failure, and (3) be a meaningful money-saver. We assume that your prime motivation for DIY work is to save money!

Each Book is a Mini-Course. While certainly nothing like a school textbook, each book in this *Professional Tips and Techniques Series* provides an in-depth treatment of the jobs it covers. Each book builds your automotive knowledge and hands-on skills. Each book prepares you to attempt new tasks and produce quality results.

A "Good Read!" We are automotive enthusiasts, and we've tried to share that love with you! We've included a lot of background info on *why* jobs are done a certain way, rather than just giving you procedures to follow blindly. We've openly shared our opinions. And we've worked hard to bring you condensed, up-to-date, and interesting information for DIY work in the 90's.

If you would like to be notified of future Do-It-Right books and videos, please send us your name and address on the enclosed form. We welcome your suggestions and comments to help us improve our books.

Dennis Holmes

Dennis Holmes
President
Do-It-Right Publishing

SHOPPING LIST

Small Dent Repairs

No dent pulling required:
- ❏ Sandpaper—40, 80, 200, 400, and 600 grit
- ❏ Body filler kit
- ❏ Filler applicators
- ❏ Mixing board
- ❏ Glazing & spot putty
- ❏ Cheese-grater file

Additional for small dent pulling:
- ❏ Suction-cup puller
- ❏ T-handle or slide-hammer puller

Larger Dent Repairs

- ❏ Slide-hammer puller
- ❏ Hammers and dollies
- ❏ Sandpaper—40, 80, 200, 400, and 600 grit
- ❏ Body filler kit
- ❏ Filler applicators
- ❏ Mixing board
- ❏ Glazing & spot putty
- ❏ Cheese-grater file
- ❏ Electric drill motor
- ❏ Flexible sanding disc
- ❏ Sanding discs—40, 200, and 400 grit

Fiberglass, ABS, & Rust Repairs

- ❏ Electric drill motor
- ❏ Flexible sanding disc
- ❏ Sanding discs—40, 200, and 400 grit
- ❏ Rust converter (rust repairs only)
- ❏ Sheet-metal snips
- ❏ Fiberglass patch kit

Painting Equipment & Supplies

For chips and scratches:
- ❏ Touch-up paint: Color Code* _____
- ❏ Touch-up primer (if required)
- ❏ Touch-up clear-coat (if required)
- ❏ Sandpaper—1000 grit (for wet sanding)

For body repairs
- ❏ Aerosol spray paint:
  Color Code* _____
- ❏ Aerosol spray primer paint:
  - ❏ Light gray ❏ Dark gray
  - ❏ Red oxide*
- ❏ Aerosol spray clear-coat (if required)
- ❏ Masking tape
- ❏ Masking paper
- ❏ Sandpaper—400, 600, and 1000 grit

General Tools & Supplies

- ❏ Flexible sanding block
- ❏ Rubbing compound
- ❏ Carnauba wax
- ❏ T-shirt or terry cloth rags
- ❏ Wax-&-silicone remover
- ❏ Tack cloth

*See page 5 for how to locate your color code.